Beyond the Valley

Mastering the Tests of Faith, Love, and Character

Archbishop Nicholas Duncan-Williams

Copyright © 2023 by Archbishop Nicholas Duncan-Williams

All rights reserved.

No part of this book may be reproduced in any form or by any electronic or mechanical means, including information storage and retrieval systems, without written permission from the author, except for the use of brief quotations in a book review.

Contents

Introduction	v
Part 1 - Test of Faith	xiii
1. Temptations and Trials	1
2. Learning from the Father of Faith	6
3. The Old Testament Titans	18
4. Other Old Testament Saints	29
5. Young Faith Icons	38
6. The New Testament Faith Holders	47
7. Make Your Faith Come Alive	57
8. Heroes of Faith in Recent History	68
Part 2 — Test of Love	81
9. In the Shadows of Love	82
10. Testing of Love in the Twilight of this World	93
11. Return to your First Love	101
12. Acts of Love for God	107
13. Acts of Love in the New Testament	115
14. Love for All People	129
Part 3 — Test of Character	141
15. The True Test of Character	142
16. Learning from Joseph	147
17. The Rigors of Righteousness	162
18. The Making of a Queen	171
19. The Mettle of Daniel	179
20. Attitudes to Watch	187
21. Modeling Christian Character	196
Prayer	209
Epilogue	211
About the Author	213

Introduction

In the grand orchestration of life, some melodies rise above the din - strains of faith, harmonies of love, and symphonies of character.

Each chord echoes within our souls, resonating through the chambers of our hearts, calling us towards something more splendid, profound, and godly. It is in these echoes, these calls from the Lord, that the framework of our lives takes shape, and we grow into the full stature of Christ.

This book explores the realms of these three pivotal virtues and seeks to guide you on an intimate journey toward understanding their intricate interplay and inherent power. We will cover these three areas in different parts of the book.

Testing of Faith

In the first part, we will look at the testing of faith. What is faith but the unwavering belief in the benevolence of Almighty God,

Introduction

trust in His infinite wisdom, and the assurance that His plans for us surpass our greatest hopes?

Yet, faith is often tested, refined like gold in the fires of life, becoming a beacon that illuminates our path. In these moments of testing, faith becomes more than just a belief; it transforms into a powerful, life-altering conviction.

The story of Horatio Spafford, an American lawyer and Presbyterian church elder, showcases the strength of faith amidst life's most severe trials.

Born in 1828, Spafford led a successful life as a lawyer in Chicago until he was confronted with a series of tragedies that would test his faith to its core. The first trial came in the form of the Great Chicago Fire of 1871, which decimated his real estate investments.

Just two years later, his faith was tested again when he sent his wife and four daughters ahead on a trip to Europe. Their ship, the Ville du Havre, was struck by another vessel and sank rapidly. All four of Spafford's daughters drowned; his wife, Anna, survived.

On his voyage to join his grieving wife, Spafford was reportedly shown the spot where his daughters' ship had sunk. Moved by intense grief and faith, he penned the lyrics to the hymn "It Is Well with My Soul," a stirring testament of faith in the face of unimaginable loss. The lyrics read:

> "When peace, like a river, attendeth my way, When sorrows like sea billows roll, Whatever my lot, thou hast taught me to say, It is well, it is well with my soul."

Despite the immense tragedies he faced, Spafford grew in

faith. He and his wife founded a Christian community in Jerusalem, dedicating the rest of their lives to missionary work. His life story is a profound testament to the power of faith during the harshest of life's trials.

Spafford became a beacon of faith in a world often clouded by doubt and despair. His life was a testament to the transformative power of tested faith, a resonating chord in the grand symphony of God's work.

Testing of Love

Love, the second melody, is the divine adhesive that binds us to each other and to God. It is a force that transcends physical barriers, breaking through walls and mending broken hearts. Yet, love, too, is put to the test. It is stretched, pulled, and sometimes torn, but it grows stronger, purer, and more resilient in those moments of trial. In its truest form, love mirrors the unfathomable depth of God's love for us.

Few personify the tested and true love more potently than Nelson Mandela. His story is one of undying love for his people, his nation, and the principle of justice.

Mandela, the first black President of South Africa, is globally renowned for his lifelong fight against apartheid. But the journey to freedom was rocky, filled with peril, and marked by profound personal sacrifice. Imprisoned for 27 years, Mandela's love for his country and his people was put to the ultimate test.

Secluded from the world, isolated from his family, Mandela's love could have easily turned into bitterness. He was put through the fire and subjected to the most brutal conditions, yet through the trials his love didn't wane. Instead,

Introduction

it took a more profound form, one of forgiveness and reconciliation.

Upon his release in 1990, Mandela carried no trace of bitterness or desire for revenge. His love, having been tested in the crucible of suffering, had transcended the confines of the ordinary, morphing into an extraordinary capacity for forgiveness.

In the ensuing years, Mandela would lead South Africa out of the dark era of apartheid, championing a new, inclusive, democratic order. His leadership was marked by a deep love, compassion, and an unwavering commitment to reconciliation. He forgave those who had imprisoned him, championed the rights of those who once suppressed him, and worked tirelessly to mend the broken bonds within his nation.

Nelson Mandela's life stands as a beacon of the transformative power of love tested by fire. His story shows that love can heal, unite, and create new beginnings even when stretched to its limits.

Test of Character

Finally, character - the symphony that echoes who we truly are. It is more than just a series of attributes or virtues; it is the essence of our being, the embodiment of our faith and love. The test of character is perhaps the most profound of all. Forged in the crucible of trials, our character ultimately shapes our destiny. It is the golden thread that weaves itself through the tapestry of our lives, determining how we respond to our tests of faith and love.

The name of Dietrich Bonhoeffer instantly springs to mind

Introduction

when contemplating believers who have demonstrated immense integrity. Born in 1906, Bonhoeffer was a German theologian, pastor, and anti-Nazi dissident during the dark era of the Second World War.

His deep faith in Christ led him to recognize the moral bankruptcy of the Nazi regime early on. He was among the first to call for the Church's explicit repudiation of Nazi policies. His bold stance included becoming a founding member of the Confessing Church, a Protestant church in Germany that arose in opposition to government-sponsored efforts to unify all Protestant churches into a single pro-Nazi Protestant Reich Church.

One of Bonhoeffer's most well-known works, "The Cost of Discipleship," reflects his understanding of the cost of standing firm in one's faith. In it, he wrote, "When Christ calls a man, he bids him come and die." This quote symbolizes the very essence of Bonhoeffer's life and the price he was willing to pay for his unflinching faith and integrity.

Bonhoeffer's commitment to the cause did not waver even when he was arrested and imprisoned in 1943 for his role in the resistance movement, including participation in a plot to assassinate Hitler. He spent two years in prison, during which he continued his writings.

His correspondence from this time, particularly his letters to his friend Eberhard Bethge, provide a powerful testament to his unwavering faith and integrity in the face of extreme adversity.

Ultimately, Bonhoeffer was executed on April 9, 1945, just weeks before the end of World War II. His integrity and steadfastness in the face of severe testing have left a lasting legacy. His life epitomizes the testing of character in the crucible of trials, demonstrating how, when grounded in faith and moral conviction, such trials can shape a person into an enduring beacon of light in the darkest of times.

Through the Fire

This book has been birthed from the quiet whisperings of my heart, the fiery furnaces of life that have tested and tempered me, and the journey that has honed my faith, deepened my love and fortified my integrity.

The path of my life and ministry has been remarkable, marked not by effortless climbs but by steep inclines, treacherous terrains, and paths paved with fire. People often ask me about the secret to my success, yearning for a quick remedy, a magical elixir that can instantly transmute their ministries into successful ventures.

However, I must tell you there are no shortcuts to enduring success. True success, the kind that extends beyond the superficial parameters of ministry size, wealth, or power, is the outcome of a soul-transforming journey. A journey that slowly and gracefully carves you into the likeness of Christ, equipping you to radiate His love in a world frayed at the seams.

Embarking on this journey means willingly stepping into the refining fires of life. There will be times when your faith will be shaken to its core, when loving those who have hurt you feels like an insurmountable task, and when compromising your integrity for fleeting success might seem like an easier path.

But it is precisely in these trying moments that you are being purified and refined. Just as gold is cleansed of impurities

Introduction

to reveal its true essence, the fire of trials strips away the layers of self so that Christ alone shines through you.

I echo the profound words of Apostle Paul (Galatians 2:20):

> "I have been crucified with Christ; it is no longer I who live, but Christ lives in me; and the life which I now live in the flesh I live by faith in the Son of God, who loved me and gave Himself for me."

In my own life, I have faced storms that raged with fury. I have been the subject of public scrutiny, my challenges splashed across the pages of national newspapers. Friends and loved ones, even those I nurtured in ministry, have turned their backs on me. I have tasted the bitterness of betrayal and known the desolation of loneliness.

In one such storm, I sought solace in the wisdom of my spiritual grandfather, the revered Evangelist Dr. T. L. Osborn. His advice to me was a beacon of light amidst the enveloping darkness.

> "Don't defend yourself. You are not on trial. If you defend yourself, you will give people the power to judge you. Never try to explain yourself...Just stay in the throne room, my son...Pursue your calling with passion as if nothing has happened."

As you journey through the pages of this book, my prayer for you is similar. May the fires of trials refine you, may your faith, love, and character shine forth brilliantly from the ashes, and may you emerge from your own crucible of fire a beacon of Christ's light in this world.

Introduction

An Invitation

This book invites you on a journey of self-discovery and discovery of God. It is a journey that will guide you through these tests, helping you understand their significance, embrace their power, and ultimately pass them with the grace and strength of the Holy Spirit.

By exploring scripture and practical life experiences, this book offers a map to navigate the treacherous, sometimes joyous, terrains of faith, love, and character.

Together, we will delve into these profound elements of our existence, exploring their depths, ascending their peaks, and traversing their valleys. We will learn from the lives of the virtuous, the faithful, and the loving. We will draw inspiration from those who have been tested and emerged triumphant and from those who have stumbled but got up stronger.

I invite you to embark on this journey with an open heart, eager to learn, willing to be shaped, and ready to be transformed. In these pages, may you find a testament of faith, a symphony of love, and a charter of character that will inspire and guide you toward a greater life of godliness.

Part 1 - Test of Faith

Chapter 1

Temptations and Trials

"It was the best of times, it was the worst of times, it was the age of wisdom, it was the age of foolishness, it was the epoch of belief, it was the epoch of incredulity, it was the season of light, it was the season of darkness, it was the spring of hope, it was the winter of despair."
 - Charles Dickens, A Tale of Two Cities

While on this Earth, we find ourselves traversing a world that seems to embody extremes. It is as if we are living within the pages of Charles Dickens' renowned novel, A Tale of Two Cities.

Prosperity and poverty walk hand in hand, while peace and war wage a perpetual battle. In certain corners of the globe, abundance and famine coexist, and love and hate paint contrasting strokes across nations. Knowledge and ignorance continue their dance upon the stage of existence. The world is a canvas upon which opposing forces collide, and we often find ourselves caught in the crossfire.

Yet, amidst this complex tapestry, hope is not lost. At the heart of it all lies a pivotal factor that tests the very essence of our virtues, both professed and possessed. It is the reality that confronts every individual, shaping our character through two distinct categories: temptation and trials.

Temptation, like a cunning serpent, slithers from within, enticing us with the allure of our own desires. Trials, on the other hand, are divine opportunities for us to prove our mettle. Temptations manipulate and deceive, while trials beckon us to handle the challenges that come our way.

In the words of James 1:13-14, we gain a deeper understanding of the perfect image of temptation:

> *"Let no one say when he is tempted, 'I am tempted by God'; for God cannot be tempted by evil, nor does He Himself tempt anyone. But each one is tempted when he is drawn away by his own desires and enticed. Then, when desire has conceived, it gives birth to sin; and sin, when it is full-grown, brings forth death."*

Temptations prey upon our innermost longings, enticing us to follow our own selfish desires. They present opportunities to obey and please ourselves. On the other hand, trials and tests provide us with opportunities to obey and please God. Temptations lead to destruction and death, while trials guide us toward the crown of life.

Temptations cloak themselves in deception, leaving us

empty and disillusioned. Trials, however, have a remarkable way of bringing the promises of God to fruition. They lead us toward wholeness, completeness, and maturity.

While temptations seek to break us down and destroy our faith, tests and trials provide fertile ground for our faith to grow, mature, and flourish.

The year 2020 served as a global examination, testing the very foundations of our beliefs and perceptions. It challenged humanity to question who truly governs the world and whether our faith in the God of the universe remains steadfast. How long can we hold onto the belief that a divine presence watches over humanity? These are the tests of faith that confronted the world.

God allowed our faith in Him to be tested. Yet, in the face of these trials, many faltered, forgetting the lessons taught before the test. They stood hollow and ill-equipped to face the circumstances that tested the very core of their faith.

As we embark on this journey of exploring the triumphs and challenges of faith, let us heed the lessons of the past. Let us embrace the tests that come our way with unwavering resolve, drawing strength from the teachings that have shaped us. In the crucible of faith, may we rise above the hollow echoes of doubt, forging a faith that withstands the fiercest trials and shines brightly amidst the darkest hours.

In the pages of this first part of the book, I aim to unveil the undeniable truth that testing our faith is not an anomaly; it is a fundamental and eternal principle that will persist as long as the earth spins on this side of eternity.

Far too often, we excuse our faltering faith by citing our

mortal nature as mere flesh and blood, expecting God to sympathize with our weaknesses. However, I am here to guide you through a captivating panorama of human beings, just like you and me, who confronted unimaginable circumstances that tested the very essence of their faith. Remarkably, they emerged victorious, standing firm in their unwavering belief.

Within these pages, you will find narratives that empower you to respond with conviction when the enemy whispers insidious lies, suggesting that your mortal nature warrants abandonment of faith in favor of a self-directed path. I invite you to embark on a transformative journey alongside individuals who, armed with faith, defied the limits of the natural and the unseen.

Their stories will ignite the flame of audacity within you, compelling you to dare to believe that every word spoken by God is true and that His promises are steadfast.

Faith, my dear reader, is a spiritual force that surges within ordinary men and women, transcending the boundaries of the physical realm.

It empowers us to rise above the limitations of the natural world, enabling us to embrace the unseen and trust in God. With faith as our compass, we possess the audacity to confront life's trials head-on, for we know that the hand of God is guiding us through the tempestuous storms.

So, prepare yourself to be captivated by tales of triumph over adversity, as we delve into the lives of those who chose to anchor their souls in faith. Let their stories embolden you to stand resolute when faced with your own tests of life.

Together, we shall navigate the depths of faith, unearthing

its boundless power and discovering the resilience that lies within us. May this journey awaken your spirit and embolden your heart, illuminating the path that leads to unwavering faith and a life that transcends the ordinary.

Chapter 2

Learning from the Father of Faith

"Faith is deliberate confidence in the character of God whose ways you may not understand at the time." - Oswald Chambers

In the ancient land of Mesopotamia, nestled between the majestic Tigris and Euphrates rivers, there lived a man named Abram. Little did he know that his unwavering faith would transform him into Abraham, forever etching his name in history as the Father of Faith.

His heart was heavy with a yearning for something more, a voice deep within him urging him to leave behind the familiar comforts of his homeland and embark on an extraordinary journey of faith.

With every step, Abraham felt the weight of the unknown pressing upon him. He had no map to guide him, no predetermined destination to strive towards. Instead, he relied solely on the voice of the One who had spoken directly into his soul, promising to lead him to a land of blessings and descendants as numerous as the stars.

As the vast desert stretched before him, the scorching sun beat down relentlessly, testing the limits of Abram's endurance. Doubt gnawed at the edges of his resolve, whispering seductively of the ease he had left behind. But Abraham, driven by an unshakeable faith, pressed on.

With each passing night, as he lay beneath a sky adorned with countless celestial bodies, Abraham would lift his gaze heavenward. The glittering stars became a testament to the promises spoken over him, a reminder of the covenant he had entered into with God.

Years turned into decades, and still, Abraham traversed the rugged terrain, clinging steadfastly to the promises of his God. His faith, once a mere flicker, had grown into a blazing fire that illuminated his path through the darkest of nights.

In due time, Abraham's faith bore fruit, as he and his wife Sarah welcomed their long-awaited son, Isaac. The promised heir, born to parents who had defied the boundaries of age and human possibility. Their joy overflowed, for they had witnessed the faithfulness of the One who had called them out of their homeland.

As we delve into the remarkable life of Abraham, we enter a world where obedience defies reason, laughter echoes with faith, and the boundaries of possibility are shattered. Brace yourself as we unravel the compelling tale of Abraham, the Father of Faith, in this chapter, unearthing timeless lessons that resonate with profound significance today.

We begin with a scriptural reference to set the stage for this remarkable story of faith:

Now it came to pass after these things that God tested Abraham and said to him, "Abraham!" And he said, "Here I am." ² Then He said, "Take now your son, your only son Isaac, whom you love, and go to the land of Moriah, and offer him there as a burnt offering on one of the mountains of which I shall tell you." ³ So Abraham rose early in the morning and saddled his donkey, and took two of his young men with him, and Isaac his son; and he split the wood for the burnt offering, and arose and went to the place of which God had told him. Genesis 22:1-2

After a series of events, God decided to test Abraham's faith. The divine voice called out to him, resonating through the air, "Abraham!" In response, Abraham dutifully replied, "Here I am."

God then uttered a command that would shake the very core of Abraham's being. "Take now your son, your only son Isaac, whom you love, and go to the land of Moriah. Offer him there as a burnt offering on one of the mountains I will show you."

Abraham, without hesitation, rose early the following day. He saddled his donkey, gathered two young men, and took his son Isaac alongside him. He meticulously prepared the wood for the burnt offering, driven by an unwavering resolve to fulfill God's command. And so, with the weight of the task heavy on his heart, Abraham embarked on this fateful journey to the place appointed by God.

The Backstory

We must delve into his backstory to truly grasp the significance of Abraham's unwavering faith. Abraham and his wife Sarah had endured years of longing, waiting for the promised child. It was God Himself who had declared that Abraham would become the father of many nations. To be worthy of such a title, one must indeed bear children. Yet, Abraham found himself in the unfortunate circumstance of being unable to conceive.

The Bible does not shy away from recounting the moment when Abraham, attempting to fulfill the promise, had a child with Sarah's maid, Hagar, and named him Ishmael. However, God made it clear that Ishmael was not the child of promise.

Only after three angels had visited Abraham and affirmed the promise of a child through Sarah did she finally bore their promised son, Isaac.

Now, just as the testimony of Isaac was being prepared to be celebrated, God introduced a perplexing and seemingly incomprehensible command. He demanded that Abraham sacrifice his beloved son, Isaac. If God had instructed the sacrifice of Ishmael, perhaps some could argue that since he was not the child of promise, his life could be offered in place of the promised child.

However, there lies a hidden truth—one that reveals the symbolic nature of the sacrifice in the grand plan of God's salvation for humanity through the eventual sacrifice of His own Son. If Ishmael were not the child of promise, his sacrifice would hold no significance for the fulfillment of God's salvation plan.

Thus, this was the ultimate test of Abraham's faith. He

believed that Isaac was a gift from God, and if he were to sacrifice him, God had the power to resurrect him or provide a worthy substitute. Yet, it was far easier to speak of such faith than to put it into action.

Abraham's faith had to reach unfathomable heights to obey this divine command. Jesus once spoke of faith as tiny as a mustard seed being able to move mountains. Then, one can only wonder at the magnitude of Abraham's faith. Did it surpass that of a mere mustard seed?

Historians suggest that Sarah's untimely death resulted from the shock she experienced when Abraham revealed the events surrounding this test of faith. How could Abraham have kept such a colossal trial from his wife, especially when they had shared in the miracle of Isaac's birth?

Here, the apex of Abraham's faith becomes evident. If this ordeal had not been a divine test and Isaac had indeed perished, what would Abraham have said upon his return to Sarah? What would have become of their lives had he chosen to disclose God's command to sacrifice their beloved son? The answer to these questions remains as elusive as it is unsettling.

The Stark Contrast

Can you perceive the stark contrast between Abraham's faith and the faith espoused in contemporary preaching?

Abraham's faith was a response to a simple command from God—an act of obedience devoid of ulterior motives, driven solely by reverence for Almighty God. It was a continuation of his unwavering trust in God, demonstrated when he departed from his homeland and family at God's behest, journeying to an unknown land that God would reveal to him.

Who would embark on such an uncertain odyssey merely because they heard a voice beckoning them to leave behind everything they held dear? Such obedience is the hallmark of one worthy of being hailed as the Father of Faith.

God did not promise Abraham that sacrificing his son would result in an abundance of progeny. In other words, this act does not align with the prevailing seed-faith principles that have permeated contemporary Christianity, often accompanied by excessive materialistic pursuits. It was a simple act of obedience to the God who possessed everything, including the special child He had bestowed upon Abraham.

Today, preachers often emphasize faith as a means to receive blessings from God. Every mention of faith revolves around acquiring something from God. Abraham, however, was distinct—he embodied a faith that transcended such desires, a faith that recognized God's sovereignty and demanded complete surrender and submission in every circumstance.

Believers today, blessed with material wealth, must ponder what holds more value: a beloved son or worldly riches.

If Abraham did not withhold his son but was willing to offer him as a sacrifice unto God, what prevents believers from trusting that investing their material blessings in the work of the ministry would be the least they could do?

Money can be regained if lost, but a lost son cannot be replaced. Learn this invaluable lesson from Abraham, and you shall embark on a transformative journey alongside the God who fashioned the universe and oversees every aspect of your life.

Distinguished within the Faith Hall of Fame

The writer of Hebrews aptly bestowed upon Abraham a distinguished position within the Faith Hall of Fame.

> *By faith Abraham obeyed when he was called to go out to the place which he would receive as an inheritance. And he went out, not knowing where he was going. By faith he dwelt in the land of promise as in a foreign country, dwelling in tents with Isaac and Jacob, the heirs with him of the same promise; for he waited for the city which has foundations, whose builder and maker is God.* Hebrews 11: 8-10

Through faith, Abraham obeyed when called to venture forth to an unknown land, a place that would become his inheritance. He resided in the promised land as a foreigner, dwelling in tents alongside his heirs—Isaac and Jacob—who shared in the same promise. His unwavering faith led him to await a city with unshakable foundations, a city whose architect and builder is God Himself.

Within these pages of the Epistle to the Hebrews, Abraham's faith is extolled further, highlighting various instances in which he exhibited unwavering trust in God in different circumstances and situations, ultimately earning him the title of Father of Faith. The writer concludes Abraham's accolades by emphasizing his recognition of heaven as the ultimate dwelling place.

Abraham's faith extended beyond the confines of his present existence. He eagerly anticipated greater promises that surpassed the temporal boundaries of life. It is truly remarkable that, thousands of years ago, Abraham's focus lay on heaven more fervently than the average believer today, who has beheld Jesus and witnessed the crucifixion unfold before their very eyes.

Do people today possess the same unwavering belief in heaven as Abraham did? Does this faith influence and dictate how they live and approach every endeavor?

Righteousness Through Faith

Let's reflect on Paul's words:

> *Therefore it is of faith that it might be according to grace, so that the promise might be sure to all the seed, not only to those who are of the law, but also to those who are of the faith of Abraham, who is the father of us all (as it is written, "I have made you a father of many nations") in the presence of Him whom he believed—God, who gives life to the dead and calls those things which do not exist as though they did;*
>
> *[1]who, contrary to hope, in hope believed, so that he became the father of many nations, according to what was spoken, "So shall your descendants be." And not being weak in faith, he did not consider his own body, already dead (since he was about a hundred years old), and the deadness of Sarah's womb.*
>
> *He did not waver at the promise of God through unbelief, but was strengthened in faith, giving glory to God, and being fully convinced that what He had promised He was also able to perform. And therefore "it was accounted to him for righteousness." Romans 4:16-22*

What sets Abraham's faith apart is his profound belief in the power and faithfulness of God. Despite facing seemingly insurmountable obstacles, Abraham placed his trust in the One who gives life to the dead and brings things that do not yet exist into existence. As prophesied, this steadfast faith allowed him to become the father of many nations.

Abraham's faith was not weakened by the natural limitations of his own body or Sarah's barrenness. Rather than dwelling on these seemingly impossible circumstances, Abraham remained resolute in his belief in God's promises. He did not waver in unbelief but found strength in his faith, giving glory to God.

What is remarkable about Abraham's faith is his complete conviction that God is able to fulfill what He has promised. Abraham's confidence in the faithfulness and power of God was unwavering. He understood that God's ability to perform His promises was not contingent upon human limitations but rooted in God's own nature.

Therefore, because of his unwavering trust and confidence in God, Abraham's faith was accounted to him as righteousness. This means that in the eyes of God, Abraham's faith was seen as a demonstration of righteousness, despite his flaws and shortcomings.

Abraham's righteousness before God was not achieved through his own merits or good works but through his unyielding faith in the character and promises of God. His faith served as the conduit through which God's grace and righteousness flowed into his life.

This biblical account of Abraham's faith provides valuable insights for believers today. It teaches us that righteousness is not attained by our own efforts or perfect behavior but by placing our trust in God and His promises. Like Abraham, we are called to believe in God's faithfulness, even in the face of seemingly impossible circumstances.

It is crucial to understand that Abraham, though mere mortal, accomplished feats that are within reach for all who walk this earth. Every individual born of a woman possesses the capacity to exercise faith in God and endure the trials that come with it. The question is, how many will pass the test when it arrives?

The Laughter of Faith: Isaac's Birth Promised

During the time when the promise of Isaac was bestowed upon Abraham, Ishmael, Abraham's firstborn with Hagar, had already turned thirteen. Abraham may have believed that Ishmael would be the long-awaited promised son. However, thirteen years after Ishmael's birth, God appeared to Abraham when he was ninety-nine years old to speak of the miraculous birth of Isaac.

Abraham, overwhelmed with astonishment, fell upon his face and laughed. He implored God, expressing his desire for Ishmael to live before the Lord. The notion of conceiving another child at the age of one hundred through his aged wife, Sarah, seemed unfathomable. Yet, the Lord reassured both Abraham and Sarah of His plans.

Abraham's laughter was the first to fill the air. It was a laugh of incredulity mingled with awe and amazement at the unfathomable nature of God's promise. Sarah, too, could not contain her laughter when God revealed His intentions.

Their laughter, however, was not a laughter of doubt but faith. Abraham's laughter resounded with a newfound understanding that defied human reasoning. Sarah's laughter was an acknowledgment that, despite her advanced age, she believed God to be faithful in fulfilling His promise.

Do Not Limit God

This episode illustrates a vital lesson: our circumstances and conditions do not limit God. His ways transcend our understanding, and His hand is not too short to accomplish what He has declared. There exists an appointed time for every breakthrough.

Patiently await your destined hour and endure the trials that come your way. Just as God declared to Moses in Exodus 9:5, "Tomorrow the LORD shall do this thing in the land," trust that He has designated a specific time for your deliverance.

The Apostle Paul, in his Epistle to the Galatians, emphasized the significance of God's timing. In the fullness of time, God sent His Son to redeem humanity (Galatians 4:4). Is anything too difficult for the Lord?

The psalmist beautifully articulated the exaltation of God's Word above all else, stating, "For thou hast magnified thy word above all thy name" (Psalm 138:2). Do not fall into the trap of limiting God. The things that seem impossible to humans are entirely possible for God (Luke 18:27).

In the crucible of faith's test, you must embrace a revelation of God's omnipotence and sovereignty. He is not bound by the limitations of mortal beings, and if He speaks, He possesses the power to fulfill His words.

Beyond the Valley

The Apostle Paul wrote to Timothy, declaring, "For I know whom I have believed and am persuaded that He is able to keep what I have committed to Him until that Day" (2 Timothy 1:12).

Until you reach a state of complete persuasion and choose to wholeheartedly believe in God, diverting your gaze from your circumstances to fixate on the Lord, you will falter in the test of faith. Be resolute in your conviction! Believe in God, and you shall establish a firm foundation for your life.

As 2 Chronicles 20:20 proclaims, "Believe in the LORD your God, so shall ye be established; believe his prophets, so shall ye prosper."

Chapter 3

The Old Testament Titans

"Faith is not the belief that God will do what you want. It is the belief that God will do what is right." - Max Lucado

The realm of faith, as epitomized by the saints of the Old Testament, is a frontier that continues to elude the grasp of contemporary Christianity. Today, faith has been reduced to a quest for divine favors, encapsulating the doctrine of seed-time, harvest, and the myriad faith principles taught.

On the other hand, the Old Testament luminaries manifested faith that acknowledged God and clung to His essence, indifferent to the trappings of material wealth or worldly acclaim. They were men and women who walked intimately with God, their lives marked by extraordinary acts of trust and obedience. These spiritual giants stood as beacons, illuminating the path of faith for generations to come.

In the preceding chapter, our gaze fell upon the titan known as the Father of Faith—Abraham. His unwavering trust in God's promises, even in the face of seemingly insurmountable odds, laid the foundation for the covenant between God and His people. Yet, Abraham's faith is only the beginning of a remarkable tapestry woven with threads of faith by the heroes of the Old Testament.

Now, we continue our journey into the lives of several more Old Testament figures, each demonstrating faith in extraordinary measures. Though separated by time and culture, these men and women share a common thread—a resolute belief in the living God and an unyielding commitment to His purpose. Through their stories, we shall witness the triumph of faith over adversity, the power of unwavering trust, and the enduring legacy of those who walk by faith, not by sight.

So, let us step back in time and allow the narratives of these Old Testament titans to ignite a flame within our souls—a flame that rekindles our faith, challenges our perspectives, and compels us to walk with the same steadfastness and courage that marked their lives. For in their journeys, we find timeless lessons, profound wisdom, and an invitation to embark on our own faith-filled odyssey, where the extraordinary awaits those who dare to believe.

The Persevering Job

The story of Job encompasses various categories of testing, whether it be testing of faith, love, or character. Let us delve into Job's remarkable journey and explore his unwavering faith amidst tremendous trials.

The narrative introduces Job as a man of immense wealth

and prosperity, a figure equivalent to today's top billionaires. Job possessed vast riches, including thousands of sheep, camels, oxen, and a large household. He was renowned as the greatest man in the East, characterized by his blameless and upright nature and deep reverence for God.

Let's look at the scriptures that start off the story of Job:

"There was a man in the land of Uz whose name was Job. This man was blameless and upright; he feared God and shunned evil. He had seven sons and three daughters, and he owned seven thousand sheep, three thousand camels, five hundred yoke of oxen and five hundred donkeys, and had a large number of servants. He was the greatest man among all the people of the East." Job 1:1-4 (NIV)

The stage was set for the testing of Job's faith. Satan, alongside the angels of God, presented himself before the Lord. God drew Satan's attention to Job, praising his blameless and upright character. Satan, however, questioned the authenticity of Job's faith, asserting that it stemmed solely from the abundance of God's blessings. Satan contended that if Job were to suffer, he would renounce his faith.

God permitted Satan to test Job, but with the condition that his life should be spared. Satan wasted no time in wreaking havoc on Job's life. In a short span of time, Job experienced the loss of his property and the tragic deaths of his children.

It is important to note that Satan's focus was not on Job's possessions but on the belief that Job's faith and commitment to God were contingent on material blessings.

Satan argued that his relationship with God would crumble

once Job's blessings were stripped away. Thus, the test was set in motion.

Job's immediate response to these calamities was awe-inspiring. Instead of succumbing to despair or blaming God, Job humbled himself before God. He tore his robe, shaved his head in mourning, and prostrated himself in worship.

> *"At this, Job got up and tore his robe and shaved his head. Then he fell to the ground in worship and said: 'Naked I came from my mother's womb, and naked I will depart. The LORD gave and the LORD has taken away; may the name of the LORD be praised.' In all this, Job did not sin by charging God with wrongdoing."* Job 1:20-22 (NIV)

Amidst his profound suffering, Job remained steadfast in his faith. He did not utter any sinful or accusatory words against God. This demonstrated his godly character, stemming from an intense and unwavering trust in God. Job's faith surpassed the realm of mere mustard seed faith; it was an unwavering belief anchored in God's love, power, and sovereignty.

However, Job's trials were far from over. Satan approached God once again, arguing that Job's physical well-being had been untouched, thus making it easier for him to maintain his faith. Satan challenged God to afflict Job's body, confident that such torment would break Job's spirit.

God granted permission, allowing Satan to inflict painful boils on Job's entire body.

Job's suffering intensified as his physical anguish combined with the grief of his earlier losses. Consumed by despair, his wife also advised him to curse God and die, leaving Job without human companionship.

Satan inadvertently gave Job one last opportunity to turn to God at that moment. Job recognized this and seized the advantage. He reasoned within himself, contemplating the inevitability of death regardless of the path he chose. Job resolved to maintain his unwavering faith in God, even if it meant persevering until his last breath.

Job defied the expectations that many would succumb to in the face of such immense adversity. He held firmly to his faith, refusing to abandon his trust in God. Consider the profound statements he made:

"His wife said to him, 'Are you still maintaining your integrity? Curse God and die!' He replied, 'You are talking like a foolish woman. Shall we accept good from God, and not trouble?' In all this, Job did not sin in what he said." Job 2:9-10 (NIV)

"Indeed, this will turn out for my deliverance, for no godless person would dare come before him!" Job 13:16 (NIV)

"I know that my redeemer lives, and that in the end he will stand on the earth. And after my skin has been destroyed, yet in my flesh I will see God; I myself will see him with my own eyes—I, and not another. How my heart yearns within me!" Job 19:23-27 (NIV)

"But if I go to the east, he is not there; if I go to the west, I do not find him. When he is at work in the north, I do not see him; when he turns to the south, I catch no glimpse of him. But he knows

the way that I take; when he has tested me, I will come forth as gold. My feet have closely followed his steps; I have kept to his way without turning aside. I have not departed from the commands of his lips; I have treasured the words of his mouth more than my daily bread." Job 23:8-12 (NIV)

Job viewed his suffering as a refining process, recognizing the opportunity for personal growth and the purification of ungodly attitudes and tendencies within himself.

Can you fathom the audacity of a man whom God boasted about for his integrity, believing that his suffering was part of a transformative process? What more remarkable testimony could this man seek?

Job's behavior starkly contrasts those who equate faith with material gain, expecting extravagant possessions like cars, houses, or private jets as signs of their faith in God. Job's faith was rooted in a profound trust in a God who is loving, powerful, and sovereign.

Despite his excruciating trials, Job maintained an unwavering belief that only God could deliver him. He placed his complete trust in God's salvation amidst his suffering. Job's faith remained unscathed, immovable, unshakable, and indestructible.

Job exhibited an attitude that defies the prevailing mindset of our time. The challenges that often lead people to abandon their faith today pale in comparison to a fraction of what Job endured. But let us remember when we question why we must endure trials and tribulations despite our faithful service to God; Job was a mere mortal, just like you and me.

When discussing unwavering faith in God, Job's example

shines brightly as a paradigm for all to witness and learn from. Are any among us prepared to pray for a faith surpassing even that of Job in our generation?

The devil may not rely on the loss of possessions or physical pain alone to test our faith in God. He may employ unexpected means, things we may not even consider.

What enabled Job to withstand the onslaught was his unwavering attitude towards God's words. In essence, his profound knowledge of God and His Word empowered him to endure the immense challenges he faced.

Job's Humanity

Job was undeniably human. He was not endowed with superhuman abilities; he experienced the same range of emotions and struggles as you and I do. At one point, his humanity became evident when he expressed his anguish and cursed the day of his birth.

In Job 3:3-14, we read Job's lamentation:

"After this, Job opened his mouth and cursed the day of his birth. And Job spoke, saying: 'May the day perish on which I was born, and the night in which it was said, "A male child is conceived." May that day be darkness; may God above not seek it, nor the light shine upon it. Why did I not die at birth? Why did I not perish when I came from the womb? Why did the knees receive me? Or why the breasts, that I should nurse? For now I would have lain still and been quiet, I would have been asleep; then I would have been at rest with kings and counselors of the earth, who built ruins for themselves.'"

Undoubtedly, Job exemplifies an extraordinary hero of faith. There can be no doubts about his unwavering devotion and resilience.

From Slavery to Lawmaker

From the clutches of slavery to the corridors of power, Moses' journey is an extraordinary testament to faith. The pivotal decision that propelled Moses to legendary status was fraught with danger, causing him to flee for his life.

The account in Hebrews 11:23-28 sheds light on Moses' remarkable faith:

> "By faith Moses, when he was born, was hidden three months by his parents, because they saw he was a beautiful child; and they were not afraid of the king's command. By faith Moses, when he became of age, refused to be called the son of Pharaoh's daughter, choosing rather to suffer affliction with the people of God than to enjoy the passing pleasures of sin, esteeming the reproach of Christ greater riches than the treasures in Egypt; for he looked to the reward. By faith he forsook Egypt, not fearing the wrath of the king; for he endured as seeing Him who is invisible. By faith he kept the Passover and the sprinkling of blood, lest he who destroyed the firstborn should touch them."

Faith is not a blind leap into the unknown; it is a conscious decision made with a clear understanding of the potential outcomes. Moses had spent nearly 40 years as an Egyptian prince, a position of great privilege and honor.

He had witnessed the splendors of Egypt, its opulent lifestyle, and the prospect of ascending to the throne as the next Pharaoh. However, he was also aware of the harsh reality of slavery, oppression, and the plight of his Hebrew brethren.

Facing this pivotal moment, Moses had to make a choice. Despite not being raised in the ways of Yahweh, when the time came for him to assert his identity, he made a decision based on faith. He looked beyond the allure of Egypt's treasures and recognized the value of suffering for the sake of God's people.

Moses esteemed the reproach of Christ as greater riches than all the wealth Egypt had to offer. He willingly chose to endure affliction alongside God's people rather than indulging in the fleeting pleasures of sin.

Sadly, many Christians today lack the fortitude to withstand afflictions. When faced with tests and trials, they falter in their faith, abandoning God and missing out on His abundant grace amidst their afflictions.

This passage portrays Moses' story of faith. It highlights how his parents, driven by faith, concealed him as an infant, recognizing his destined purpose. It also illustrates how, by faith, Moses relinquished wealth, power, and prestige to walk the path of humility.

At that time, Moses was unaware of the Ten Plagues, the miraculous crossing of the Red Sea, and the subsequent events that would solidify his status as a biblical icon. He valued suffering for the sake of God more than attaining godlike status in Egypt.

It is essential to distinguish the faith exhibited by the saints of old from the faith-talk prevalent in modern Christendom. Their faith was not centered on obtaining material blessings from God; instead, it stemmed from their unwavering trust in God for who He is and His faithfulness to His word.

When considering the remarkable life of Moses, as testified by God Himself, and the incredible works God accomplished through him over the span of forty years, it should come as no surprise.

Moses did not commence his journey as the lawgiver of Israel, nor did he anticipate becoming an iconic figure associated with the crossing of the Red Sea. It never crossed his mind that he would stand alongside Jesus Christ during the glorious transfiguration, representing the Law as Elijah represented the Prophets.

We must reflect upon our choices and contemplate what we value above the wealth of Job or the fame of Moses, who rose to power from the status of a slave boy in a foreign land, much like Joseph did in Egypt.

May we earnestly pray for God to raise giants of faith in our generation and future generations should Jesus delay His second coming.

Phases of Testing

The phases of Moses' test of faith were numerous and challenging. Time and again, he was called upon to confront Pharaoh and demand the release of God's people, relying on the display of God's power through miracles and plagues.

However, each encounter with Pharaoh resulted in disappointment as the Egyptian king stubbornly refused to let the Israelites go. This ongoing test of faith, where victory seemed within reach only to be met with resistance, must have taken a toll on Moses. Nevertheless, he faithfully returned to Pharaoh every time God commanded him to do so.

Throughout his journey, Moses also faced the prospect of rejection from his own people. He wondered if the Hebrews would accept him as their leader and believe that God had sent him.

After all, he had been a fugitive who disappeared from their midst for forty years. Yet, despite his past, Moses had to trust in God's ability to use him. He had to overcome the constant rejection of his leadership and maintain his faith as he led the Hebrews through the wilderness, relying on God for miraculous provision and supernatural manifestations. Despite countless trials, Moses remained steadfast in his faith and held on to God.

These challenges prompt us to reflect on our own ability to trust God in the face of unrelenting resistance from the enemy. Can we continue to trust God even when the situation remains unchanged or reverts back to its previous state, even after faithfully carrying out all that God has asked of us? It is in these moments of unwavering trust that our faith is truly tested.

Chapter 4

Other Old Testament Saints

"Faith consists in believing when it is beyond the power of reason to believe." - Voltaire

Amidst the sweeping narratives of kings and prophets in the Old Testament, lies a fabric of faith woven by saints whose stories may have been overshadowed by the giants of biblical history. Their lives may not have spanned countless chapters, but their unwavering faith and remarkable encounters with God carry profound significance for us today.

These unsung heroes of faith beckon us to explore the depths of their stories, to peer through the corridors of time, and to witness their encounters with God. Within their seemingly ordinary lives, we uncover extraordinary lessons that transcend the boundaries of time and culture, resonating with the core of our own human experience.

Let us delve into their narratives, extract timeless truths

from the scriptures, and discover practical applications that can inspire and empower us in our own journeys of faith.

Abel's Test

Hebrews 11:4 tells us of Abel's faithful offering to God, which was more excellent than that of his brother Cain. Through this act of faith, Abel obtained a witness that he was righteous, and God testified of his gifts.

Remarkably, even after Abel's untimely death at the hands of his brother, his legacy continues to speak to us spiritually. It serves as a reminder that our good works have the power to testify long after we are gone.

The test of faith presented in Abel's story revolves around the issue of trust. Will we rely on our own ways, logic, and reasoning to find solutions, or will we trust in God's ways? We can discern this through the contrasting sacrifices of Cain and Abel. The narrative describes Abel's offering as excellent, but what made it more excellent than Cain's?

To unravel the depth of this question, let us return to the story of Adam and Eve. When our first parents sinned in the garden, they attempted to cover their nakedness with fig leaves, relying on their own efforts. However, God intervened and clothed them with the skins of animals—a foreshadowing of the need for a sacrificial system.

Unlike Cain, Abel placed his faith in God's redemptive solution to humanity's problem. He offered a sacrificial animal, acknowledging his need for God's atoning grace. On the other hand, Cain followed his parents' example and trusted in his own human endeavor, offering produce from the ground as a means of atonement and restoration. Cain's trust resided in human reasoning and logic, while Abel's faith rested in God's prescribed procedure.

Despite God's admonition to Cain to do what is right, he chose to be wise in his own conceit and ultimately committed the grave sin of killing his brother Abel.

Trusting in God is a recurring theme throughout the entire Bible. Let us glean wisdom from the following scriptures:

"Trust in the LORD with all thine heart; and lean not unto thine own understanding. In all thy ways acknowledge him, and he shall direct thy paths." Proverbs 3:5-6

"Be not wise in thine own eyes: fear the LORD, and depart from evil." Proverbs 3:7

"Seest thou a man wise in his own conceit? there is more hope of a fool than of him." Proverbs 26:12

"He that trusteth in his own heart is a fool: but whoso walketh wisely, he shall be delivered." Proverbs 28:26

The test of faith ultimately comes down to a matter of trust. Will you trust God and follow His path, or will you lean on your own understanding?

Challenging times will put your faith to the test, requiring you to trust in God's instructions even when they do not make sense to your finite mind. It means relying on God rather than relying on yourself for a solution.

The Test of Noah's Faith

> *By faith Noah, being warned of God of things not seen as yet, moved with fear, prepared an ark to the saving of his house; by the which he condemned the world, and became heir of the righteousness which is by faith.* Hebrews 11:7

Hebrews 11:7 rightfully acknowledge Noah in God's Faith Hall of Fame.

God warned him of a catastrophic flood, something that had never been witnessed before, and he responded with faith. Driven by reverence and awe, Noah faithfully constructed an ark to save his household. Through obedience, he condemned the world's unbelief and became an heir of righteousness through faith.

Imagine being entrusted with an unprecedented assignment—one that defies the limits of human imagination and comprehension. Noah was tasked with building an ark to prepare for a flood that would devastate the earth.

For years, Noah endured ridicule as he embarked on this monumental project. Can you fathom the jeering, mockery, name-calling, and insults he faced as he diligently built the ark and called people to repentance?

Undoubtedly, there were moments when Noah questioned whether he truly heard from God.

What about his wife and children? How did they perceive their husband and father amidst the ridicule and opposition? While the Bible does not provide explicit details, we can only imagine the challenges Noah and his family encountered.

However, the fact that we are reading Noah's testimony today and that Jesus Himself referred to Noah when speaking of the signs preceding His second coming attests to Noah's faithfulness. Noah passed the test.

Will you stand firm in your faith when others mock your assignment and ridicule what the Lord has called you to do? Can you believe God for something new that challenges the norms of your world, even when you cannot comprehend its rationale?

Faith often leads us to appear foolish in the eyes of those who rely solely on logic and human reasoning—especially in our present post-modern, humanistic society that places man at the center of affairs. If you prioritize your reputation over obedience to God's leading, you will falter in the test of faith.

Enoch's Test

> *By faith Enoch was translated that he should not see death; and was not found, because God had translated him: for before his translation he had this testimony, that he pleased God.* Hebrews 11:5

Hebrews 11:5 declares that Enoch was translated so that he would not see death. He pleased God because he walked with Him, according to Genesis 5:24.

Verse six of Hebrews 11 further illuminates the testing element of Enoch's faith, explaining that without faith, it is impossible to please God. Those who come to God must believe that He exists and that He rewards those who diligently seek Him.

What happens when we walk with God? The answer is found in the prophet Amos's vital question: "Can two walk together, except they be agreed?" (Amos 3:3). Walking with someone necessitates agreement on various aspects such as location, meeting time, destination, route, and pace.

Note that Enoch's distinction lies in the Bible, stating, "Enoch walked with God." The scripture does not say that God walked with Enoch. This implies that Enoch relinquished the decision-making power concerning timing, location, pace, and destination to God. He trusted God to set the agenda and faithfully walked at God's pace, so to speak.

How often do we trust God regarding these points of agreement?

Your test of faith may manifest in the area of patience. Can you hold on to faith when there appears to be a delay? When God's pace and timing seem too slow for your desires, and you yearn to run when God says, "In My time"? Scripture reminds us, "He that believeth shall not make haste" (Isaiah 28:16).

Many Christians today seek for God to align with their whims rather than aligning themselves with God. Jesus Himself proclaimed, "Nevertheless not as I will, but as thou wilt" (Matthew 26:39). Similarly, in John 5:30, Jesus declared, "I seek not mine own will, but the will of the Father which hath sent me."

To agree with God is to rely on Him, trust His character, and acknowledge that His choices, ways, and dealings are always superior. Enoch agreed with God on God's terms, pleasing Him by allowing God—not himself—to set the course, direction, and destination. Enoch counted on God.

Elijah's Test

The story of Elijah in 1 Kings 18:41-45 portrays a testing of his faith in God. It says:

> *And Elijah said unto Ahab, Get thee up, eat and drink; for there is a sound of abundance of rain.*
>
> *So Ahab went up to eat and to drink. And Elijah went up to the top of Carmel; and he cast himself down upon the earth, and put his face between his knees,*
>
> *And said to his servant, Go up now, look toward the sea. And he went up, and looked, and said, There is nothing. And he said, Go again seven times.*
>
> *And it came to pass at the seventh time, that he said, Behold, there ariseth a little cloud out of the sea, like a man's hand. And he said, Go up, say unto Ahab, Prepare thy chariot, and get thee down that the rain stop thee not.*
>
> *And it came to pass in the mean while, that the heaven was black with clouds and wind, and there was a great rain. And Ahab rode, and went to Jezreel.*
>
> *And the hand of the Lord was on Elijah; and he girded up his loins, and ran before Ahab to the entrance of Jezreel.*

Israel had turned away from God and followed the prophets of Baal. Elijah prophesied that there would be no rain for seven years—a consequence of their disobedience. When the time for rain finally arrived, Elijah approached King Ahab and declared the imminent arrival of abundant rainfall.

However, the rain did not immediately pour upon the earth despite Elijah's prayer. He sent his servant seven times to check for any sign of rain, but each time the report was disheartening—there was nothing. Nevertheless, Elijah persisted, instructing his servant to go again seven times.

"Go again seven times," Elijah declared, unwavering in his faith and continued prayer.

What about You?

Can you endure repeated resistance and unfulfilled expectations? Do you possess the confidence that, regardless of how many times you are rejected, opposed, resisted, laughed at, frustrated, or disappointed, God will come through?

Looking closely at the story shows that Elijah did not give up. He remained steadfast in prayer until the rain finally descended upon the earth. Similarly, Moses faced a similar test when he approached Pharaoh—ten times he went, believing God for a turnaround. In the test of faith, will you persist until you witness the manifestation of God's Word?

Today, many Christians are quick to revert to the "ways of Egypt" when faced with challenges in their walk with God. They abandon their faith community when their hopes and expectations are unmet and their faith is stretched thin.

However, these accounts of Old Testament saints—Abel, Noah, Enoch, and Elijah—speak directly to us, encouraging us to persevere, trust God, and remain faithful amid trials. Their stories remind us that faith is eternally relevant and not confined to a specific era or generation.

Let their testimonies inspire us to fully trust God, relinquishing our own understanding and embracing His ways. Let us seek His will, follow His leading, and trust that He rewards those who diligently seek Him. The tests of faith we encounter may differ, but the principles of trust, obedience, and unwavering commitment remain constant.

As we navigate our journeys of faith, let us remember the words of Proverbs 3:5-6: "Trust in the LORD with all thine heart; and lean not unto thine own understanding. In all thy ways acknowledge him, and he shall direct thy paths."

May our faith be unwavering, our trust unyielding, and our commitment resolute as we walk the path set before us, inspired by the examples of these faithful saints of the Old Testament.

Chapter 5

Young Faith Icons

"Faith is the strength by which a shattered world shall emerge into the light." - Helen Keller

In the grand tapestry of faith, we often find ourselves drawn to the stories of seasoned saints who have weathered the storms of life, standing firm in their unwavering trust in God.

We marvel at the faith of Abraham, who believed in the promise of a son even in his old age, and the unwavering determination of Moses, who led the Israelites out of bondage through the parted waters of the Red Sea. These giants of faith inspire and encourage us, but they also seem distant, their experiences far removed from our own.

But what about the young ones? What about those whose faith was tested in the fire of youth, who stood for truth and righteousness when the weight of the world pressed against them?

In this chapter, we turn our gaze to a group of young faith icons—youth trained in the Hebrew Scriptures and found themselves far from their homeland, captives in the land of Babylon.

Their stories are less widely known than those of Abraham or Moses but are equally significant. These young men faced trials that tested the very core of their beliefs, and in their unwavering faith, they shine as beacons of hope and inspiration for us today.

They did not have the luxury of negotiating on behalf of cities or witnessing God's faithfulness over decades. Their faith was tested in the crucible of Babylon, surrounded by a culture that sought to erase their heritage and replace it with foreign gods and customs.

Imagine being ripped from your homeland, your family, and everything you hold dear, only to find yourself immersed in a society that sought to brainwash you, to strip away your faith in the one true God. Such was the reality for these young faith icons.

They were enrolled in schools where the literature and language of the Chaldeans were taught—knowledge that stood in stark contrast to the truths they had been raised on.

Yet, in the face of this tremendous pressure, they remained steadfast.

They refused to bow down to the idols of Babylon, even when threatened with fiery furnaces and a den of lions. Their stories are not just accounts of unwavering faith; they are reminders that even amid darkness, God's light shines brightest through the hearts of those who are young and committed to Him.

Their journeys will inspire and challenge us, igniting a fire within our hearts to stand firm in our faith, regardless of the circumstances surrounding us. So, let us learn from their unwavering commitment, drawing strength and courage to face the trials of our own lives with boldness and unwavering trust in God. In their stories, we find that age is not a prerequisite for extraordinary faith, and youth can be a powerful catalyst for change in a world desperately needing God's truth.

Let us delve into their story as it unfolds in Daniel 1:1-4:

> "In the third year of the reign of Jehoiakim king of Judah, Nebuchadnezzar king of Babylon came to Jerusalem and besieged it. And the Lord gave Jehoiakim king of Judah into his hand, with some of the articles of the house of God, which he carried into the land of Shinar to the house of his God; and he brought the articles into the treasure house of his God. Then the king instructed Ashpenaz, the master of his eunuchs, to bring some of the children of Israel and some of the king's descendants and some of the nobles, young men in whom there was no blemish, but good-looking, gifted in all wisdom, possessing knowledge and quick to understand, who had the ability to serve in the king's palace, and whom they might teach the language and literature of the Chaldeans."

These young men found themselves in a foreign land where they and their families had been taken as captives. It is crucial to understand the context of their faith test. The king of Babylon had a clear agenda for these young men—to indoctrinate them with the language and literature of the Chaldeans.

This literature was not derived from the Torah or borrowed from the Hebrews. It was designed to erase any memory of

Yahweh from their minds. The first step in this process was changing their names to Babylonian ones.

> *"Now from among those of the sons of Judah were Daniel, Hananiah, Mishael, and Azariah. To them the chief of the eunuchs gave names: he gave Daniel the name Belteshazzar; to Hananiah, Shadrach; to Mishael, Meshach; and to Azariah, Abed-Nego."* Daniel 1:6-7

Each of the Hebrew names carried meanings connected to their faith in God. For example, Daniel means "God is my judge," with the suffix -el referring to Elohim, one of the names of the God of Israel.

Azariah and Hananiah have the suffix -iah or -yah, shortened forms of Yahweh, the covenant name of God. These changes were intended to detach them from their Hebrew roots and assimilate them into the ways and gods of Babylon.

Similarly, the names given to their friends were associated with Babylonian deities. This change of their names marked the beginning of their test.

To Defile or Not to Defile

The first test of their faith came in the form of their refusal to eat the king's delicacies and drink his wine.

> *"But Daniel purposed in his heart that he would not defile himself with the portion of the king's delicacies, nor with the wine which he drank; therefore he requested of the chief of the eunuchs that he might not defile himself. Now God had brought*

Daniel into the favor and goodwill of the chief of the eunuchs. And the chief of the eunuchs said to Daniel, 'I fear my lord the king, who has appointed your food and drink. For why should he see your faces looking worse than the young men who are your age? Then you would endanger my head before the king.'"
Daniel 1:8-10

While some may consider this a minor issue, it was a significant matter for these young men. It announced their faith in God in the face of something contrary to their beliefs—a test they passed.

By abstaining from the king's delicacies, they demonstrated their allegiance to God. Their faithfulness did not go unnoticed, for they were found healthier at the end of the testing period than those who ate from the king's portion.

To Bow or Not to Bow

Another major test confronted three of these young men. We read in Daniel 3:4-6:

> *"Then a herald cried aloud: 'To you it is commanded, O peoples, nations, and languages, that at the time you hear the sound of the horn, flute, harp, lyre, and psaltery, in symphony with all kinds of music, you shall fall down and worship the gold image that King Nebuchadnezzar has set up; and whoever does not fall down and worship shall be cast immediately into the midst of a burning fiery furnace.'"*

The history does not provide clear information on how

many years of indoctrination these young men had undergone. However, their unwavering faith in the face of intense adversity becomes evident.

Despite the threat of being cast into a fiery furnace, they refused to bow down to the golden image. It was a momentous decision—one that required immense courage.

Consider what it says in Daniel 3:16-19:

"Shadrach, Meshach, and Abed-Nego answered and said to the king, 'O Nebuchadnezzar, we have no need to answer you in this matter. If that is the case, our God whom we serve is able to deliver us from the burning fiery furnace, and He will deliver us from your hand, O king. But if not, let it be known to you, O king, that we do not serve your gods, nor will we worship the gold image which you have set up.' Then Nebuchadnezzar was full of fury, and the expression on his face changed toward Shadrach, Meshach, and Abed-Nego. He spoke and commanded that they heat the furnace seven times more than it was usually heated."

Their response to the king was an act of profound faith. They were not merely exercising faith to receive something from God; instead, they demonstrated their unwavering commitment to God Himself.

They had been taught the history of their forefathers, from Abraham to Moses and David, which was replete with accounts of God's miraculous interventions. Their faith, therefore, was not solely based on the hope of miraculous deliverance from the fiery furnace but on a deep-seated trust in God's power and sovereignty.

They were willing to die for what they believed in. Death by fire stared them in the face, offering life if only they bowed before a lesser god. Yet, they chose death rather than compromise their faith.

Their actions were grounded in the commandment, "You shall not bow down to any graven image." This resolute stand for their faith in the most challenging circumstances should inspire us in our world, where ideologies, philosophies, and human attitudes often oppose God and His Word.

To Pray or Not to Pray

The final test of faith involved Daniel himself. Out of envy and jealousy, conspirators sought to discredit him because of his favor with the king. They found an opportunity in Daniel's commitment to pray to God. As it says in Daniel 6:6-9:

> "So these governors and satraps thronged before the king and said thus to him: 'King Darius, live forever! All the governors of the kingdom, the administrators and satraps, the counselors and advisors, have consulted together to establish a royal statute and to make a firm decree that whoever petitions any god or man for thirty days, except you, O king, shall be cast into the den of lions. Now, O king, establish the decree and sign the writing, so that it cannot be changed, according to the law of the Medes and Persians, which does not alter.' Therefore King Darius signed the written decree."

Notice how the proposal pleased the king, who failed to recall the incident with Daniel's three friends. He signed the decree, which prohibited anyone from praying to any deity except the king for a period of thirty days.

Daniel had every opportunity to show loyalty to the king. In this case, it was not an open test of bowing before an image. Some might argue that it was an opportunity to be wise, temporarily suspending prayer for that month and then resuming their prayers. However, Daniel chose a different path. He continued to pray three times a day. His faith faced a severe test, as the consequences for defying the decree were dire.

Daniel's unyielding faith prevailed. Even though the king respected Daniel in his heart for his excellence and wisdom, the king struggled with Daniel's defiance of the decree, as it challenged his authority.

Nonetheless, Daniel upheld his faith, knowing that the Lion of Judah surpasses all lions, just as He is King above all kings, including Nebuchadnezzar himself. We all know the outcome—the Lord delivered Daniel from the lions' den, and the king continued to honor him.

Let us pray that God raises up even greater individuals of faith in this generation, eagerly awaiting the rapture. These young faith icons serve as examples for today's youth, who often find themselves preoccupied with matters that do not please God or honor Him before the world.

May we be inspired by the unwavering faith of these young men who faced trials that tested the very core of their beliefs. Their example encourages us to stand firm in our faith, regardless of the challenges we encounter in a world that often opposes God's ways. Through their stories, we see the power and faithfulness of God, who honors those who remain steadfast in their devotion to Him.

As we navigate our own journeys of faith, let us remember these Youth Faith Icons, drawing strength and inspiration from their unwavering commitment to God. Their stories remind us that faith is not confined to age or experience; it is an unwavering trust in God's promises and a willingness to stand firm even in the face of adversity. May their stories encourage us to embrace our own faith tests, knowing that God is faithful and will honor those who put their trust in Him.

Chapter 6

The New Testament Faith Holders

"Trials teach us what we are; they dig up the soil, and let us see what we are made of."
- Charles Spurgeon

The New Testament may not provide an extensive compilation of stories akin to the Old Testament saints who withstood great tests of faith. Nevertheless, within its pages, we find glimpses and teachings illuminating the importance of unwavering faith in challenging circumstances.

As we embark on this journey, let us remember that faith, even in the New Testament context, differs from the modern-day perception that often equates faith with personal gain and blessings.

The faith of these saints was rooted in a deep acknowledgment of who God is, surpassing the desire for external possessions and worldly accolades. Their unwavering trust in God set them apart and paved the way for extraordinary testimonies of faith.

The Parable of the Widow

In the parable of the widow before the Lawyer, Jesus emphasizes the significance of persistent prayer and the necessity of holding firm to faith amid unfavorable situations.

In Luke 18:1-8, we encounter the story:

> *"Then He spoke a parable to them, that men always ought to pray and not lose heart, saying: 'There was in a certain city a judge who did not fear God nor regard man. Now there was a widow in that city; and she came to him, saying, "Get justice for me from my adversary." And he would not for a while; but afterward he said within himself, "Though I do not fear God nor regard man, yet because this widow troubles me I will avenge her, lest by her continual coming she weary me." ' Then the Lord said, 'Hear what the unjust judge said. And shall God not avenge His own elect who cry out day and night to Him, though He bears long with them? I tell you that He will avenge them speedily. Nevertheless, when the Son of Man comes, will He really find faith on the earth?'"*

In this parable, a widow approached a judge who neither feared God nor respected other people—a strikingly familiar scenario in the corrupt landscape of the 21st century.

How does one navigate the presence of a powerful individual who holds the key to what you seek? Such individuals are ubiquitous in our world, and dishearteningly, some even profess belief in God or claim to be Christians.

Take note of the question Jesus posed at the end of the parable. When the Son of Man returns, will He find faith on the earth? Will there be a group of people who unwaveringly believe in God, regardless of the tumultuous circumstances that unfold? Will there be believers who, like the young shepherd David, fearlessly face giants, seeing them as mere dogs defiling the armies of the living God?

How will your faith in God as the provider of breakthrough endure in the face of such individuals? This was the test of the widow's faith, prompting Jesus to share this parable.

If you persevere and refuse to give up, God, who holds every heart in His hands, knows how to touch and soften even the hardest of hearts that stand in the way of your progress.

In any endeavor involving the will of human beings, our ultimate reliance lies in the Holy Spirit, who can tenderize even the most callous hearts. Where else can we earnestly pray for this transformation than when leading a congregation of fallen and redeemed men and women?

It may be easy to boast of a congregation with thousands of members on television, but the true measure lies in the number of hearts genuinely committed to God. How many exercise faith in God, holding onto it as the widow clung to hers until the judge granted her request?

If you find that your faith as a pastor, concerning what you desire to see in your congregation, is under attack, remember the parable of Jesus and never cease approaching the courts of heaven on behalf of your flock.

Jesus declared that God would surpass the actions of the

corrupt judge. Yet, He posed the million-dollar question: When the Son of Man returns to the earth, will He find such faith?

Our present world is plagued by corruption, where reverence for the Lord and the conviction of conscience have faded in many hearts. It is a harsh reality we must confront and arm ourselves against. Let us not allow the attitudes of corrupt individuals to shake our faith in God or cause us to doubt His very nature.

If you have entered into a covenant with God, you possess the ability to conquer anything. That is precisely what the enemy seeks to attack. He gains the upper hand if he can erode your faith in God and lead you to doubt the Scriptures.

However, as long as we maintain faith and continue to speak, declare, and pronounce the truths in God's Word, we will always emerge victorious. Our faith is the key that unlocks the door to the supernatural, enabling us to overcome every obstacle that hinders our journey of faith.

Jesus Prayed for Peter's Faith

In a significant discussion with Peter, Jesus brings to light a crucial aspect of faith. Luke 22:31-34 records this exchange:

> "And the Lord said, 'Simon, Simon! Indeed, Satan has asked for you, that he may sift you as wheat. But I have prayed for you, that your faith should not fail; and when you have returned to Me, strengthen your brethren.' But he said to Him, 'Lord, I am ready to go with You, both to prison and to death.' Then He said, 'I tell you, Peter, the rooster shall not crow this day before you will deny three times that you know Me.'"

It is evident from Satan's intentions that his primary focus in coming against Peter was to attack his faith. The adversary employs the same tactic with every child of God we have studied thus far.

Satan does not directly target your finances or possessions, as demonstrated in the story of Job, where he failed. Instead, he aims for your faith. The enemy knows that once he undermines your faith in God, he has achieved his purpose and will move on to the next saint to bring down.

Recognizing this, Jesus assured Peter that He had prayed for him, interceding that his faith would remain steadfast and unwavering.

If we fast-forward to the trial of Jesus, we can understand why Jesus specifically prayed for Peter's faith. Peter denied knowing Jesus three times before the rooster crowed, as Jesus had foretold. Jesus was aware that Peter's faith would be tested, for Peter was destined to become the leader of the Apostles. The fulfillment of that divine plan hinged on Peter's faith in Jesus standing firm.

Thankfully, we know that Peter's faith was ultimately restored. As we continue to the book of Acts, we witness a transformed Peter who boldly questioned the Sanhedrin, asking whether it was right to obey man rather than God. Such was the power of Jesus' prayer for Peter's faith.

It comes as no surprise, then, that Peter himself speaks of faith as something precious. In 1 Peter 2:6-9, he writes,

> *"In this you greatly rejoice, though now for a little while, if need be, you have been grieved by various trials, that the genuineness of your faith, being much more precious than gold that perishes,*

though it is tested by fire, may be found to praise, honor, and glory at the revelation of Jesus Christ, whom having not seen you love. Though now you do not see Him, yet believing, you rejoice with joy inexpressible and full of glory, receiving the end of your faith—the salvation of your souls."

If Jesus Himself found it necessary to pray for Peter's faith, then faith must surely be treasured.

As we have followed the events from biblical times until now, we recognize faith's immeasurable value. Each of us has the extraordinary opportunity to build our faith to the point where it becomes unshakable, for we live in times of severe testing.

The intensity of the trials that lie ahead cannot be predicted. Thus, it becomes all the more crucial that we pray for one another so that our faith may stand firm collectively.

It is one thing to read about faith but another to truly believe and live it out. Whether we attend church regularly or not, any action taken without faith is considered sin.

Whenever we fail to act in faith, we act in fear—fear of the circumstances unfolding in the world and how they might impact us.

"The just shall live by faith," means that without faith, we cease to truly live; we merely exist. Without faith, we wither away. This is why Jesus emphasized the importance of having faith in God. The truth is that everyone possesses a measure of faith.

"For I say, through the grace given to me, to everyone who is among you, not to think of himself more highly than he ought to

think, but to think soberly, as God has dealt to each one a measure of faith." Romans 12:3

There is no one who does not have faith. Every individual has been given a measure of faith. Whether your faith is small, weak, or great, let it be reflected in your response to the Word of God. As you exercise your faith, even if it starts small, it will grow to the magnitude of the faith held by Job, Daniel, Moses, and the saints of old.

Hebrews 11:6 reminds us, *"But without faith it is impossible to please Him, for he who comes to God must believe that He is and that He is a rewarder of those who diligently seek Him."*

What the enemy is after in your life is not your possessions or achievements but your faith. If you lose everything and maintain your faith in God, you will bounce back. However, if the enemy attacks your faith and succeeds in taking it away, you cease to truly live and merely exist. That is why you must have faith that God exists. God rewards faith, and what we are currently facing is a test of our faith.

Allow me to help you strengthen your faith. Consider the sequence of night and day within 24 hours. Evening comes first, followed by the morning. The greater light—the sun—was created for the day. Weeping endures for the night, but joy comes in the morning. If the greater light is designed for the day, it stands to reason that times of joy will surpass periods of darkness.

Do not belittle the faith you have in God. Release it when necessary. Faith is the only thing that, when released, you do not lose; instead, you gain even more.

How the Death of the Early Followers of Jesus Demonstrate Faith

In this final section of this chapter, I would like to highlight the remarkable faith demonstrated by the early followers of Jesus through the manner of their deaths:

1. **Peter and Paul:** Both Peter and Paul were martyred in Rome around 66 AD during Emperor Nero's persecution. Paul was beheaded, while Peter, out of humility, requested to be crucified upside down as he deemed himself unworthy to die in the same manner as his Lord.

2. **Andrew:** Tradition holds that Andrew was martyred by crucifixion in the Greek city of Patras around 60 AD. Like his brother Peter, Andrew did not consider himself deserving of the same death as Jesus. Consequently, he was bound, rather than nailed, to a cross in an X shape, now known as Saint Andrew's Cross. Andrew also ventured to the "land of the man-eaters" in what is presently Russia, where Christians credit him as the first to bring the gospel. He preached in Asia Minor and Greece, and it is believed he was ultimately crucified.

3. **Thomas:** Thomas likely carried out his ministry mainly in the regions east of Syria. Tradition suggests that he traveled as far as India, where the ancient Marthoma Christians consider him their founder. According to their accounts, he was martyred when pierced with the spears of four soldiers.

4. **Philip:** Philip possibly had a significant ministry in Carthage, North Africa, and later in Asia Minor. It is said that he converted the wife of a Roman proconsul, resulting in his arrest and cruel execution.

5. **Matthew:** Known as the tax collector and author of

Beyond the Valley

the Gospel of Matthew, ministered in Persia and Ethiopia. The accounts regarding his death vary, with some reports stating that he was not martyred, while others claim he was stabbed to death in Ethiopia.

6. **Bartholomew:** Tradition attributes widespread missionary travels to Bartholomew, including India alongside Thomas, Armenia, Ethiopia, and Southern Arabia. His martyrdom is narrated in various accounts, with the most prevalent tradition suggesting he was flayed and beheaded. This is why artwork often depicts him holding or wearing his own skin or associating him with flaying knives.

7. **Saint James:** James, the son of Zebedee, was the first of Jesus' apostles to be martyred for his faith, and his death is recorded in the Bible. He was executed by the sword under the rule of King Herod, who sought to please the Jews and prevent the spread of Christianity.

8. **James:** This James, the son of Alpheus, ministered in Syria. The Jewish historian Josephus reports that he was stoned and then clubbed to death.

9. **Simon the Zealot:** Simon ministered in Persia and was killed for his refusal to sacrifice to the sun god.

10. **Matthias:** Chosen to replace Judas Iscariot as an apostle, Matthias is said to have traveled to Syria with Andrew. Tradition holds that he died by burning.

11. **John:** John is the only apostle widely believed to have died a natural death from old age. He served as the leader of the church in the Ephesus region and is known for caring for Mary, the mother of Jesus, in his home. During Domitian's persecution in the mid-90s AD, John was exiled to the island of Patmos, where he wrote the book of Revelation. According to an early

Latin tradition, John miraculously survived being immersed in boiling oil in Rome, leading to the conversion of the entire coliseum witnessing the event.

The deaths of these early followers of Jesus testify to their unwavering faith, even in the face of severe persecution and gruesome executions. Their examples are powerful reminders of the depth of commitment and conviction they possessed, inspiring generations of believers to stand firm in their faith regardless of the challenges they may face.

Chapter 7

Make Your Faith Come Alive

"God's work done in God's way will never lack God's supply." - Hudson Taylor

Imagine yourself standing in the middle of a fierce battlefield. The air is tense as the enemy launches relentless attacks from every direction. Doubt, fear, and uncertainty surround you, threatening to undermine your faith and leave you vulnerable to defeat.

But in the midst of this chaos, there is a powerful weapon at your disposal—the Word of God.

When you face trials and tribulations, the enemy will do everything in his power to shake your faith. He will whisper lies and plant seeds of doubt, hoping to cripple your confidence in God's promises. But in these moments, you have a choice—to succumb to the enemy's tactics or to rise up in faith and declare the truth that sets you free.

The practice of faith is not a passive endeavor. It requires active participation and unwavering commitment. Just as an athlete trains diligently to excel in their chosen sport, you too must train your faith muscles to withstand the onslaughts of doubt and fear. In the daily practice of speaking and declaring God's Word, your faith comes alive and gains the strength to overcome any obstacle.

Heaven-mindedness and Faith

The Scriptures reveal to us the hidden secret of how the saints of old were able to hold on to their faith amidst challenging earthly circumstances—they were consumed by a heavenly perspective. This truth is eloquently conveyed in Hebrews 11:13-16:

> *"These all died in faith, not having received the promises, but having seen them afar off were assured of them, embraced them and confessed that they were strangers and pilgrims on the earth. For those who say such things declare plainly that they seek a homeland. And truly if they had called to mind that country from which they had come out, they would have had opportunity to return. But now they desire a better, that is, a heavenly country. Therefore, God is not ashamed to be called their God, for He has prepared a city for them."*

Regrettably, we have yet to fully grasp the power and significance of this truth. In our relentless pursuit of material possessions and earthly comforts, we have overlooked the transformative impact of having a heavenly mindset.

The distorted emphasis on prosperity has distorted our

vision of heaven, causing many Christians to become disillusioned and resort to desperate measures in their quest for wealth and success in this temporary life rather than standing firm in their faith when faced with earthly challenges.

The apostle Paul echoed this perspective in his letter to the Corinthians, urging them to fix their minds on heavenly things:

> *"Therefore we do not lose heart. Even though our outward man is perishing, yet the inward man is being renewed day by day. For our light affliction, which is but for a moment, is working for us a far more exceeding and eternal weight of glory, while we do not look at the things which are seen, but at the things which are not seen. For the things which are seen are temporary, but the things which are not seen are eternal."* 2 Corinthians 4:16-18

There awaits a heavenly realm that far surpasses this present life's temporary pleasures and struggles. We must shift our focus and allow the influence of heaven to shape our faith on Earth.

Though they may seem overwhelming, the afflictions we face in this world are but a light burden compared to the immeasurable glory that awaits us. The joy that is set before us surpasses the darkness that surrounds us.

Even when the morning seems distant and the night appears endless, we must hold on to the certainty that the morning will come. It is a test, and we shall pass it, emerging with a testimony. There is no room for negotiation or compromise in this matter.

Therefore, let us rise above the distractions and enticements of this world, fixing our gaze on the eternal realities of heaven.

As we embrace a heaven-mindedness, our faith will come alive, invigorated by the assurance of the promises that await us. May our hearts be filled with the unwavering conviction that the glories of heaven far outweigh the fleeting pleasures of this earthly existence. Let us walk in the footsteps of those who have gone before us, faithfully holding on to their faith, and may our lives bear witness to the transformative power of heavenly perspectives.

Practicing Your Faith

During the COVID-19 pandemic, I found myself in a situation where I had dinner with someone who later tested positive for the virus. Concern and fear tried to creep into my thoughts, whispering that the virus would surely get me. I had to combat those negative voices daily by declaring God's Word over my life.

Indeed, during times like these, we must adhere to the protocols and guidelines put in place for our safety. It is essential to exercise wisdom and caution. However, we must not allow ourselves to place our faith solely in these protocols rather than in God, our ultimate healer of all diseases.

This statement is not meant to undermine the importance of following protocols; it is a reminder to anchor our faith in God amidst our challenges. No human has all the answers, and the duration of the virus remains uncertain.

Perhaps, one day, we will wake up to the news that COVID-19 has vanished. We will acknowledge God's love, faithfulness, and deliverance on that day. Until then, let us hold fast to our faith in Him.

I am not suggesting that we act recklessly, but I urge you to have faith in God's Word. When your faith is tested during this pandemic, you must exercise faith for healing. I am not referring to mere positive thinking; I am speaking of a deep-seated faith in what God accomplished through Christ's sacrificial love demonstrated at Calvary.

These are undoubtedly difficult and trying times. Yet, in the face of adversity, we have the potential to accomplish more than we ever have before. The Holy Spirit spoke to me, saying, "A thousand shall fall at thy side." And He asked me, "Nicholas, do you believe?" In response, I declare, "Lord, I believe!" Whenever voices of doubt and fear assail me, I shout, "Lord, I believe!"

Sometimes, you may fast and pray diligently, and your situation worsens rather than improves. The enemy may try to convince you that your prayers are in vain. At this point, you must boldly declare God's Word even more resolutely.

You have the power to dismantle every attack on your faith. Whatever the enemy has thrown at your faith, it must be dismantled. Break through the enemy's fiery darts that seek to diminish your faith.

Speak the Word

It is written in 2 Corinthians 4:13, "And since we have the same spirit of faith, according to what is written, 'I believed, and therefore I spoke,' we also believe and therefore speak."

God's instructions are clear. You must never cease speaking the Word.

Speak the Word into every situation that confronts you. When Satan points out your past failures, speak the Word.

When he presents seemingly insurmountable circumstances, speak the Word. Even when he haunts you with the threat of death, you have one powerful weapon at your disposal—continue to speak the Word.

Let the spirit of faith arise within you. Believe in God's promises, declare His Word boldly, and watch as your faith comes alive, overcoming every obstacle. The challenges we face today are no match for our indomitable faith in Christ.

You must also understand that Satan rarely gives up. He continually tests your faith in God, seeking to lower your guard. Therefore, it is essential to continue speaking the appropriate Word of God.

In 2 Samuel 5:17-19; 22-23, we read about how the Philistines launched a comeback against David after he was anointed as king over Israel. David sought the face of the Lord and inquired if he should go up against the Philistines. The Lord assured David of victory, saying, "Go up, for I will doubtless deliver the Philistines into your hand."

This is what I call Satanic reinforcement and demonic comebacks. Just like David faced opposition from the Philistines, you may also encounter situations where the enemy tries to bring back old habits, temptations, or struggles. When you find the enemy attempting to resurrect your past, it is a sign that he has nothing new to attack you with—these are demonic comebacks.

Never underestimate the stubbornness of the enemy. Any stubborn situation must be dismantled in the name of Jesus. Whatever lies in wait for you, let it be dismantled and scattered. Do not tolerate anyone seeking to steal your joy or hinder your testimony. Speak God's Word with authority!

This is not a time to be complacent or passive. Command the forces of darkness to scatter. Use the Word of God, just as Jesus did. If you believe, declare it boldly. Speak forth the promises of God and proclaim victory over every attack.

Fellowship with Other Believers

In Romans 10:17, we learn that faith comes by hearing and hearing by the Word of God. It is through hearing the Word that faith is stirred within us. This is precisely why the enemy does not want believers to gather together. When we come together as the body of Christ, we hear God's Word, and our faith is strengthened.

That is why the writer of Hebrews warns against the behavior of Christians who cease to fellowship with other believers. Some may stop attending church because they have experienced prosperity, while others may stop coming because their desired financial blessings did not manifest as expected. It is crucial to recognize the importance of gathering together, for it is in these times of collective worship and teaching that we receive the Rhema—specific words spoken to specific individuals at specific times for specific purposes.

Therefore, in the face of demonic comebacks and challenges, let us hold fast to our faith and continue speaking the Word of God. May our faith be ignited and sustained through hearing and declaring His promises.

And as we gather together in unity, let our faith be strengthened as we receive the specific Word of God for our lives.

As Hebrews 10:25 advises, "Let us not neglect our meeting together, as some people do, but encourage one another, especially now that the day of his return is drawing near."

And in Psalm 133:1, it says, "How good and pleasant it is when God's people live together in unity!" By gathering together, we can uplift and support one another, growing in faith as we navigate life's challenges.

Triumphs of Faith

The triumphs of faith are evident throughout history, as we see in the accounts shared in Hebrews 11:31-38. These stories testify to the power of faith and its ability to bring about extraordinary victories.

One such triumph is exemplified in the story of Rahab, the harlot who showed faith by receiving the spies with peace. When the city of Jericho was destroyed, Rahab and her family were spared because of her faith and obedience. She chose to align herself with God's people and was saved from destruction along with them.

The list of triumphant faith continues with the names of renowned individuals like Gideon, Barak, Samson, Jephthah, David, Samuel, and the prophets. These men of faith subdued kingdoms, demonstrated righteousness, and obtained the promises of God.

Their faith enabled them to conquer formidable foes and overcome significant challenges. They witnessed divine intervention in stopping the mouths of lions, quenching the violence of fire, and escaping the edge of the sword.

In weakness, they found strength, and they became valiant in the face of battle. They turned armies of aliens into flight, leaving their enemies defeated and bewildered. Women witnessed their dead loved ones being raised back to life through their faith.

However, the triumph of faith is not limited to deliverance from physical trials. Some believers endured persecution and chose not to accept deliverance as they longed for a better resurrection. These faithful ones endured torture, cruel mocking, scourging, imprisonment, and even death. They remained steadfast in their faith, knowing their ultimate reward awaited them in eternity.

The world was not worthy of these faithful individuals who wandered in deserts, and mountains, and sought refuge in dens and caves of the earth. They were destitute, afflicted, and tormented, yet their faith remained unshaken. Their perseverance in the face of immense hardship testifies to the depth of their faith and their unwavering trust in God.

Beloved, understand that God has ordained your victory in the test of faith. The foundation of this triumph is rooted in your belief that Jesus is the Son of God. This confession of faith is the underlying confidence that carries you through every battle and test. As John writes in 1 John 5:4-5, "For whatever is born of God overcomes the world. And this is the victory that has overcome the world—our faith. Who is he who overcomes the world, but he who believes that Jesus is the Son of God?"

Embrace the triumphs of faith as your own. Let the stories of those before you inspire and encourage you. Draw strength from their examples and recognize that the same faith that carried them to victory is available to you today. Through faith in Jesus Christ, you can conquer every obstacle, withstand every trial, and emerge triumphant in the face of adversity. Place your trust in Him, for He is faithful to fulfill His promises and lead you to victory.

How Their Faith Impacts Us

The examples set by the Old Testament saints and the early New Testament believers are a powerful testimony to their unwavering faith.

Their faith was not driven by earthly desires or personal gain but rather by a deep belief in God Himself. They understood that true faith transcended material possessions and worldly accomplishments.

The saints of old did not pursue faith to acquire lavish mansions or extravagant luxuries. Their faith was not about displaying their wealth or seeking worldly recognition. They focused on God and His Word, trusting in His promises and placing their hope in the heavenly rewards that awaited them.

The early followers of Jesus in the New Testament era exemplified this same faith. They faced persecution, trials, and even death for their unwavering commitment to Christ. Their faith was not swayed by the allure of worldly success or the fear of earthly suffering. They lived with the expectation that their ultimate portion was in the heavenly realms.

As we reflect on their lives, let us not underestimate the significance of their faith and its impact on our own journey of faith. We must be cautious not to bow our heads in shame when we stand alongside these faithful men and women in heaven. Their testimonies should inspire us to cultivate a genuine and unyielding faith in God, not driven by selfish desires or worldly pursuits.

Beyond the Valley

In our own lives, let us remember that true faith goes beyond superficial displays and empty rituals. It is a faith deeply rooted in a personal relationship with God. It is a faith that sustains us in the face of adversity, empowers us to overcome challenges, and fuels our hope in the eternal promises of God.

May we strive to emulate the faith of these saints, placing our trust in God and His Word above all else. Let our faith be a testimony that withstands the test of time and stands as a shining example to those who come after us.

As we continue our journey of faith, may we walk in the footsteps of these faithful saints, knowing that our ultimate gathering with them in heaven will be a joyous and glorious occasion, free from shame and filled with the joy of fellowship in the presence of our loving God.

Chapter 8

Heroes of Faith in Recent History

"Afflictions add to the saint's glory. The more the diamond is cut, the more it sparkles; the heavier the saints' cross is, the heavier will be their crown." - Thomas Watson

Throughout history, extraordinary individuals have walked among us, men and women whose lives radiate with the brilliance of unwavering faith. Like beacons of light in a world shrouded in darkness, their stories inspire us to embrace the limitless possibilities that faith in God can unleash.

As we delve into the final chapter of this book's first part, we embark on a journey through recent history, exploring the lives of remarkable individuals who embodied the very essence of faith. Though not recorded in the ancient scriptures, their stories echo the faith of those celebrated in Hebrews 11. Through their unwavering belief in the face of adversity, they blazed a trail of inspiration that continues to guide us today.

Martin Luther

In the annals of history, amidst the challenges and triumphs of faith, a remarkable story emerges from the last 500 years—the inspiring tale of Martin Luther. Born in Eisleben, Germany, in 1483, Luther became a pivotal figure in the Protestant Reformation.

As a young man, Luther embarked on a quest for revelation, diligently studying the Scriptures and seeking solace in his devout Catholic faith. However, as he delved deeper into the teachings of the church, he grew increasingly disillusioned by what he perceived as corruption and a departure from the true essence of Christianity.

In 1517, Luther's convictions reached a tipping point when he penned his famous Ninety-Five Theses, challenging the practices of indulgences and calling for reform within the Catholic Church. His act of defiance sparked a wildfire of controversy, setting in motion events that would forever change the course of religious history.

Facing intense scrutiny and opposition from the church hierarchy, Luther remained resolute in his convictions, driven by an unwavering faith in God's truth. His bold stand ignited a theological revolution and became a testament to the power of unwavering faith in the face of formidable adversity.

Luther's journey was fraught with trials and tribulations. He faced excommunication, condemnation, and threats to his very life. Yet, throughout it all, his faith remained steadfast. With each passing challenge, he clung fiercely to believing that God's Word held the ultimate authority, and that true salvation came through faith alone.

In the face of immense pressure and opposition, Luther's unwavering faith propelled him forward. His determination to uphold the truth and restore the essence of Christianity birthed a movement that would forever shape the Christian landscape.

William J. Seymour

Another pioneer of faith in modern history, who, amidst the trials and adversities of the early 20th century, shone brightly as a beacon of faith, is William J. Seymour. Born in 1870 in Centerville, Louisiana, Seymour would become a key figure in the Azusa Street Revival, a movement that would revolutionize the landscape of Christianity.

Seymour's journey was marked by perseverance and an unyielding commitment to his faith. As an African-American man in a deeply segregated society, he faced systemic racism and discrimination daily.

Despite the obstacles before him, Seymour clung tightly to his belief in the power of the Holy Spirit to break down barriers and bring unity among believers.

In 1906, Seymour found himself in Los Angeles, where he became the pastor of the Azusa Street Mission. It was within the humble walls of this small building that a spiritual fire was ignited, leading to one of the most significant revivals in modern Christian history.

The Azusa Street Revival was characterized by an outpouring of the Holy Spirit, with signs and wonders accompanying the preaching of the Gospel. People from diverse backgrounds, including different races and social classes, gathered to seek God's presence and experience the power of the Holy Spirit.

However, Seymour's faith was not without its challenges. Many people rejected the revival, viewing it as strange and unconventional. The racial integration at Azusa Street was particularly controversial, as it went against the deeply ingrained prejudices of the time. Yet, Seymour remained steadfast, firmly believing that the love of Christ could transcend societal divisions and bring unity among believers.

As the revival gained momentum, news of Azusa Street spread far and wide, drawing people from across the United States and even from other countries. The meetings were marked by spiritual manifestations, such as speaking in tongues, healing, and prophetic utterances. Despite the skepticism and opposition, Seymour stood unwavering, placing his trust in the power of God to transform lives and bring about a spiritual awakening.

Seymour's faith amid adversity was not just confined to the revival meetings. He exemplified a life of humility, simplicity, and prayer, seeking God's guidance and relying on His strength in every circumstance. His unwavering commitment to the Gospel and his passion for the Holy Spirit's work ignited a revival that would have a lasting impact on the global Christian community.

The Azusa Street Revival sparked a renewed hunger for spiritual revival and a deeper experience of the Holy Spirit in the lives of believers. It laid the foundation for the Pentecostal and charismatic movements that continue to shape Christianity to this day.

Corrie ten Boom

Born in the Netherlands in 1892, Corrie ten Boom and her family lived a life dedicated to their faith in Christ and providing shelter for those in need.

During the dark days of World War II, as Nazi occupation engulfed their beloved country, the ten Boom family transformed their home into a secret refuge for Jews and members of the Dutch resistance. They risked their lives to save countless individuals from the clutches of the enemy.

However, in 1944, their courageous acts of compassion were discovered, and the ten Boom family was arrested. Corrie, along with her father and sister, was sent to a concentration camp, enduring unimaginable hardships, and witnessing the atrocities of the Holocaust.

Throughout her harrowing ordeal, Corrie clung to her unwavering faith, finding solace and strength in her belief that God's love and goodness would prevail, even in the darkest circumstances. She became a source of light and hope to her fellow prisoners, sharing the message of God's unfailing love and forgiveness, even towards their captors.

Amid desolation and despair, Corrie's faith became a guiding compass, leading her to demonstrate extraordinary forgiveness and grace. Despite her immense suffering, she chose to forgive those who had perpetrated unspeakable acts, embodying the transformative power of faith in the face of profound evil.

Following her release from the concentration camp, Corrie dedicated her life to spreading the message of God's love and forgiveness. She became a renowned author and speaker, sharing her remarkable story and inspiring others to embrace a faith that transcends the boundaries of pain and adversity.

Smith Wigglesworth

Within the last century, the life of Smith Wigglesworth stands as a testament to the power of unwavering faith. Born in 1859 in Yorkshire, England, Wigglesworth experienced a profound transformation that would shape the course of his life and impact countless others.

In his early years, Wigglesworth was not known for his faith. He worked as a plumber and lived a life marked by rebellion and indifference towards God. However, everything changed when his wife, Polly, encouraged him to attend a Salvation Army meeting. During that gathering, Wigglesworth encountered God's life-altering presence, and from that moment forward, his life would never be the same.

As Wigglesworth delved into the teachings of the Bible, a fire ignited within him—a fire fueled by a relentless faith that defied all odds. He became known for his boldness and unwavering belief in God's miraculous power to heal and transform lives.

Throughout his ministry, Wigglesworth's faith was tested time and again. He encountered opposition, skepticism, and even ridicule from those who doubted the validity of his claims. Yet, undeterred, he pressed on, fully convinced that God's power was not limited by human understanding or skepticism.

Countless testimonies bear witness to the remarkable miracles that occurred through Wigglesworth's ministry. He prayed for the sick, and they were healed. The blind received sight, the deaf heard, and the lame walked. His ministry became synonymous with supernatural manifestations, as he believed wholeheartedly in the power of God to overcome every obstacle and bring forth extraordinary breakthroughs.

But Wigglesworth's faith was not limited to physical healing alone. He was deeply convinced that God's power extended to all aspects of life, including spiritual transformation. He fervently preached the message of repentance and the need for a personal encounter with Jesus Christ, knowing that true change and salvation came through faith in Him.

What set Wigglesworth apart was not just the miracles he witnessed or the crowds he drew but the unyielding nature of his faith. He refused to compromise or water down the truth of the Gospel. He believed in the power of God's Word to transform lives and bring about lasting change.

Kathryn Kuhlman

Kathryn Kuhlman, a renowned evangelist of yesteryear, possessed a faith that not only transformed countless lives but also endured the test of time and adversity. Her remarkable journey inspires believers worldwide, demonstrating the power of unwavering faith even in the face of profound testing.

Throughout her ministry, Kuhlman faced numerous trials and challenges that tested the depth of her faith. She encountered skepticism and criticism from both within and outside the church and endured personal battles and health struggles. Yet, it was during these moments of testing that Kuhlman's faith shone brightly, revealing her strength and resilience.

One of the most significant tests of Kuhlman's faith

occurred when she experienced a season of apparent barrenness in her healing ministry. For a time, the miraculous healings she had become known for seemed to diminish, leaving her grappling with doubt and uncertainty. Rather than allowing despair to take hold, Kuhlman turned to God in fervent prayer, seeking His guidance and wisdom.

During this testing period, Kuhlman's faith was refined and deepened. She realized that her ministry was not about her own abilities or performances but wholly dependent on God's grace and power. This revelation made her surrender even more fully to God's will and trust in His timing and purposes.

As Kuhlman yielded to God's leading, her ministry experienced a revival and an outpouring of God's healing power. Countless individuals received physical, emotional, and spiritual healing through her ministry, and the impact of her faith became a beacon of hope for those in desperate need.

Kuhlman's faith was characterized by an unwavering belief in the miraculous and supernatural. She firmly held that God was not limited by human understanding or circumstances. Her faith propelled her to step out boldly, despite skepticism and doubt, as she believed that God's power was available to transform lives and bring about divine healing.

Benson Andrew Idahosa

Benson Andrew Idahosa, widely known as the "Father of Pentecostalism" in Nigeria, had a faith that endured time, adversity, and cultural opposition. His life and ministry serve as a powerful example of how unwavering faith can overcome seemingly insurmountable challenges and transform lives.

Born into a humble family in Benin City, Nigeria, Idahosa faced significant obstacles from an early age. He grew up in a culture steeped in traditional beliefs and practices, with Christianity viewed as a foreign religion. However, even as a young boy, Idahosa exhibited a hunger for God and a desire to know Him more intimately.

As he embraced his faith and embarked on his journey as a minister, Idahosa encountered intense testing and opposition. His unyielding belief in the power of God's Word and the reality of the supernatural clashed with his community's prevailing skepticism and religious traditions. Yet, rather than being deterred, Idahosa remained resolute, convinced that God had called him to bring a message of hope and transformation to his people.

One of the most significant tests of Idahosa's faith occurred when he faced severe financial challenges early in his ministry. With limited resources and societal expectations stacked against him, he found himself in a position where his faith was stretched to its limits.

However, rather than succumbing to doubt or compromising his convictions, Idahosa clung to God's promises and refused to waver in his belief that God would provide for his needs.

In the face of financial adversity, Idahosa's faith became the catalyst for miraculous provision. Through a series of remarkable encounters and divine interventions, he witnessed God's faithfulness as financial resources were supernaturally multiplied, debts were canceled, and doors of opportunity were opened. These experiences testified to the reality of God's provision and the power of unwavering faith.

Beyond financial challenges, Idahosa also faced opposition and persecution for his bold proclamation of the Gospel. He encountered resistance from traditional religious leaders, government authorities, and even fellow Christians who questioned his methods and teachings.

Yet, in the face of adversity, Idahosa stood firm in faith and the leading of the Holy Spirit.

His ministry became a catalyst for the growth of Pentecostalism in Nigeria and the broader African continent. Through crusades, conferences, and the establishment of churches, Idahosa's unwavering faith in the power of the Gospel brought about transformation and healing in the lives of countless individuals.

Idahosa's faith was marked by audacity, a refusal to accept the status quo, and an unwavering belief in the supernatural power of God. His life and ministry demonstrated that faith is not just an abstract concept but a tangible force that can shape destinies and bring about societal change.

The testing of Idahosa's faith refined and strengthened him, allowing him to become a powerful instrument in the hands of God. Each challenge he faced became an opportunity to demonstrate his unwavering trust in God's faithfulness and his unwavering belief in the power of the Gospel.

His legacy continues to inspire generations of believers to step out in audacious faith, confront cultural and societal norms, and embrace God's supernatural power. Through his example, Idahosa reminds us that faith is not passive but active, and it requires us to take bold steps and trust God's leading even in the face of testing and opposition.

David Yonggi Cho

David Yonggi Cho, the founder of Yoido Full Gospel Church in Seoul, South Korea, is a remarkable example of unwavering faith and its transformative power.

From humble beginnings to becoming one of our time's most influential spiritual leaders, Cho's journey is a testament to the boundless possibilities that arise when faith takes root in the human heart.

Cho's faith was deeply rooted in his relationship with God and his unwavering belief in the power of prayer. From the early days of his ministry, he embraced the concept of "cell groups," small gatherings where believers could come together to pray, study the Bible, and support one another. Through these intimate settings, Cho witnessed the transformative power of faith in the lives of individuals and the growth of his congregation.

One of the defining moments of Cho's faith journey came when he faced a seemingly insurmountable challenge. In the 1960s, Yoido Full Gospel Church experienced a period of stagnation, with a congregation of only 50 members. But Cho refused to succumb to despair.

Instead, he prayed fervently to God, seeking guidance and direction. During this time, Cho received a revelation about the 4th dimension (faith), the power of the Holy Spirit, and the necessity of a life rooted in prayer that would forever change the course of his ministry and build the largest church in the world.

With a renewed sense of purpose and an unshakeable trust in God's faithfulness, Cho embarked on a mission to share the revelation that God gave him. Under Cho's leadership and unwavering faith, Yoido Full Gospel Church experienced an incredible revival. The congregation began to grow exponentially, attracting thousands of believers.

Cho's faith extended beyond the church walls as he embraced a vision for social impact and community development. He initiated various humanitarian projects, including establishing the Kookmin University and creating programs to alleviate poverty and provide education and healthcare to marginalized communities. Cho believed that true faith must be accompanied by action and tangible expressions of love for others.

Cho faced various challenges and criticisms throughout his ministry, yet his faith remained unshaken. He firmly believed in the power of God's promises and the potential within each individual to overcome obstacles through faith. His teachings on faith, prayer, and spiritual warfare continue to inspire millions of believers worldwide to embrace a deeper level of trust in God and the limitless possibilities that faith unlocks.

Lessons Learned

From the lives and legacies of Martin Luther, William Seymour, Corrie ten Boom, Smith Wigglesworth, Kathryn Kuhlman, Benson Idahosa, and David Yonggi Cho, we glean invaluable lessons that transcend time and culture.

Collectively, the lives of these individuals reflect vital principles that shape our faith and influence our walk with God. Their unwavering commitment to truth, the pursuit of unity, forgiveness, radical faith, sensitivity to the Holy Spirit, impactful leadership, and visionary prayer challenge us to deepen our relationship with God, embrace His transformative power, and impact the world around us.

May their examples inspire us to seek God's guidance, step out in audacious faith, and boldly proclaim the Gospel, leaving a lasting legacy of faith for generations to come.

Part 2 – Test of Love

Chapter 9

In the Shadows of Love

"Love recognizes no barriers. It jumps hurdles, leaps fences, penetrates walls to arrive at its destination full of hope." - Maya Angelou

In the ebb and flow of human existence, we find ourselves suspended between moments of extreme delight and desolation, wisdom and folly, faith and skepticism, enlightenment and obscurity, hope and despair.

Just as Charles Dickens' nuanced depiction of a tumultuous era in "A Tale of Two Cities" struck a chord in the first part of our exploration of the test of faith, it continues to echo in this second part on the test of love. Like Dickens' narration, our lives are a tapestry of dichotomies woven together, reflecting a complex ballet of contrasting experiences.

But amidst this oscillating narrative of human history, one element remains unwavering and transcendent - the love of God.

His love cuts through the best and worst of times, transforming the age of foolishness into wisdom, turning incredulity into belief, flooding the season of darkness with light, and turning the winter of despair into the spring of hope.

In this divine love, we anchor our exploration, tracing its imprints in the grand narrative of creation, its persistence throughout human history, and its ultimate manifestation in the act of salvation.

As we journey through this chapter, may you find your own story intersecting with the greater narrative of God's love, and may you encounter the depth of His affection in both the heights of joy and the depths of despair. For God's love is as steadfast during the worst of times as it is during the best of times. His love loved us first.

God Commands Us to Love Him

God's command to love Him is also a testament to His unfathomable love for us. In Jeremiah 31:3, God declares: "I have loved you with an everlasting love; I have drawn you with unfailing kindness." It's a sublime symphony, a melodious echo of the divine relationship between the Creator and the created, filled with grandeur and majesty, intimacy, and affection.

When we examine the framework of our earthly relationships, we can witness the manifestation of this divine commandment in various forms. For instance, consider the unblemished affection between a mother and her newborn child. The mother, tired and drained from the tribulations of labor, musters the strength to hold her infant, her eyes filled with infinite love. It's pure, unconditional, and transcends all boundaries. This gives us a glimpse of the kind of love God asks us for.

Similarly, think of the farmer tending his fields under the searing sun, his brow bathed in sweat and body aching with fatigue. However, he labors on, nurturing every seed with love and care, guided by the dream of an abundant harvest. His relationship with his land is akin to our relationship with God – it calls for unwavering commitment, patience, and sincere love. As such, he mirrors the essence of Deuteronomy 6:5, where we are commanded to love the LORD with all our heart, soul, and strength.

> *"Hear, O Israel: The Lord our God, the Lord is one! You shall love the Lord your God with all your heart, with all your soul, and with all your strength. Deuteronomy 6:4-5*

In our daily lives, we encounter numerous situations where we must choose between God and worldly pleasures. At times, our human instincts may gravitate towards the latter.

Take, for example, a busy corporate professional who continually finds herself absorbed in her work, missing church services, neglecting her prayer life, and sidelining her spiritual nourishment for worldly gains. The constant struggle to balance her love for God with her ambition in a materially-driven world vividly illustrates the challenges we face in our commitment to loving God.

There's a poignant story in the gospel of Luke where a rich young ruler, despite adhering to all commandments, finds it hard to give up his wealth to follow Jesus:

And behold, a certain lawyer stood up and tested Him, saying, "Teacher, what shall I do to inherit eternal life?" He said to him, "What is written in the law? What is your reading of it?" So he answered and said, " 'You shall love the Lord your God with all your heart, with all your soul, with all your strength, and with all your mind,' and 'your neighbor as yourself.' " And He said to him, "You have answered rightly; do this and you will live."
Luke 10:25-28

His love for material possessions surpassed his love for God, thus revealing the profundity of Jesus' command in Matthew 10:37 that our love for God must supersede all other loves. It's a stark reminder that our worldly possessions are transient, and our love for God is the only enduring love that brings eternal joy.

In stark contrast, let us consider the story of Job, who never ceased to love God amid tremendous suffering. Job's wealth, children, and health were all stripped away, leaving him in a pit of despair. Yet, he continued loving God, demonstrating an unshakeable faith and love for his God. Job's story shows that even in our darkest moments, our love for God becomes a beacon of hope, guiding us back to light.

From these examples, we can glean that God doesn't merely command us to love Him but beckons us to step into an unending relationship filled with devotion and affection. This love is not a theoretical construct; it requires practical and conscious action, just like Jesus's command in John 14:15 - 17.

"If you love Me, keep My commandments. And I will pray the Father, and He will give you another Helper, that He may abide

with you forever— the Spirit of truth, whom the world cannot receive, because it neither sees Him nor knows Him; but you know Him, for He dwells with you and will be in you.

In essence, loving God is a journey of constant discovery, of learning to transcend our human desires and surrender ourselves to the will of God. Like a river that tirelessly carves through mountains to meet the ocean, our love for God requires resilience and determination. It is not a matter of obligation but an outpouring of gratitude for His abiding love.

The choice to love God entails a deep and purposeful commitment, a life anchored in unwavering faith, and a spirit filled with adoration for our Heavenly Father. To love God is to listen, obey, trust, and hope in Him, even when circumstances challenge these convictions. To love God is to consciously put Him at the center of our lives, nurturing a relationship that transcends the confines of time and space, echoing into eternity.

As we progress in our spiritual journey, remember that the command to love God is not an arbitrary decree from a divine overlord but an invitation to a fuller, more profound, and more enriching life. As we learn to love God with all our heart, soul, mind, and strength, we also learn the true meaning of being human, for we were created out of love, by Love Himself, to love.

God's Love in Creation

God's love is a foundational truth that we can see painted in vivid colors in the creation narrative. The meticulously crafted Earth, the well-orchestrated sequence of creation, the carefully

Beyond the Valley

designed beings – everything testifies of a Creator who is not only infinitely powerful but also profoundly loving.

The Book of Genesis presents a sublime portrayal of divine love in action. Each day of creation was a thoughtful and intentional act driven by love and purpose. God, the divine Potter, shaped the universe, imparting form and function to all that exists. With every stroke of His divine brush, He painted a canvas of love, providing the perfect dwelling place for His masterpiece – humankind.

In the swirling galaxies and spinning planets, in the vibrant colors of sunrise and the hushed whispers of the night, in the diverse species of flora and fauna, in every gust of wind and drop of rain, God was laying out His love for us, setting the stage for His unwavering act of love – the creation of human beings.

When God said, "Let us make man in our image, after our likeness" (Genesis 1:26), He was not merely talking about our physical form but also about our capacity to love, create, dream, and foster relationships. He declared His love for us, a love so profound that He wanted to share His divine nature with us, to let us be His representatives on Earth.

Each act of creation was a testament to His deep affection and meticulous care for us. He provided us with an abundant Earth ripe with resources to nourish and sustain life. He created vast oceans, towering mountains, fertile plains, and myriad creatures to ensure we had everything necessary for a fulfilling life. He did not just provide for our survival but also for our joy, painting the world with colors and filling it with melodies and fragrances.

In God's creation, we see the ultimate expression of sacrificial love, a love that thinks first of the beloved's welfare rather than what it can gain. In stark contrast, human love often tends to be self-centered, focusing on personal gain rather than the well-being of the other. But God's love is different. His love is selfless, generous, and unchanging.

Love often calls for respect, understanding, and care in our human relationships. We respect those we love, care for their well-being, and strive to understand them better. God, in His infinite love, bestowed upon us the highest honor – He made us co-creators with Him, entrusting us with the stewardship of the Earth. He respected our free will, understanding our need for purpose and growth.

When God commanded us to "Be fruitful and multiply, fill the earth and subdue it" (Genesis 1:28), He was not just delegating authority but expressing His confidence in us. He showed us respect and entrusted us with a mission close to His heart. This responsibility should inspire us to value and protect God's creation, understanding that our actions directly affect the world around us.

Indeed, God's love shines through every aspect of creation, every blade of grass, every ray of sunshine, every drop of water. It calls us to a deeper awareness of His constant presence, unending care, and boundless love for us. God loved us first, and He loved us well. As we walk through life, let us be ever mindful of His love, reflecting it in our interactions with others and our stewardship of His creation.

God's Love in Human History

From the moment God breathed life into Adam to the culmination of biblical history, we see a divine narrative of unending love. God, in His infinite mercy, has always stayed by man's side, guiding, protecting, and loving, even when man turned his back on Him. This love is perfectly encapsulated in the words of Jesus as recorded in Matthew 5:43-46.

> *"You have heard that it was said, 'You shall love your neighbor and hate your enemy.' But I say to you, love your enemies, bless those who curse you, do good to those who hate you, and pray for those who spitefully use you and persecute you, that you may be sons of your Father in heaven; for He makes His sun rise on the evil and on the good, and sends rain on the just and on the unjust. For if you love those who love you, what reward have you? Do not even the tax collectors do the same?* Mathew 5:43-46

Jesus' revolutionary concept of love demonstrates God's endless love for us all. Unlike our limited human perspective, which often conditions love on reciprocal affection and can even harbor disdain for perceived enemies, God's love is universal and unconditional. He loves us irrespective of our stance toward Him.

The rain that nourishes the crops and the sunshine that warms the Earth do not distinguish between the righteous and the unrighteous. These blessings are God's gifts to all. They are given freely and equally to all, even to those who doubt or deny His existence.

Suppose we question God's love based on specific challenges or setbacks. In that case, we focus narrowly on a fraction of the picture while overlooking the myriad blessings He showers upon us daily.

In challenging times, we may question God's love for us. But when those trials pass, we often acknowledge His love again. Logically, shouldn't we recognize His love even during difficult times? God's love is constant and unchanging, even though we, as humans, may struggle to understand and accept it.

God's Love in Salvation

The greatest demonstration of God's love is found in the sacrifice of His Son on the cross. Jesus' crucifixion was not merely a display of God's power; it was an act of unfathomable love, intended to rescue humanity from the relentless grip of evil.

In the gospel of John, we find the profound exchange between Jesus and Nicodemus, where Jesus reveals His divine mission. Jesus assures Nicodemus—and all of humanity—that whoever believes in Him will not perish but have everlasting life.

> *For God so loved the world that He gave His only begotten Son, that whoever believes in Him should not perish but have everlasting life. For God did not send His Son into the world to condemn the world, but that the world through Him might be saved.* John 3:16-17

No declaration of love in human history can match the depth and breadth of God's love as expressed in this passage.

The Apostle Paul further elucidates this divine love in his letter to the Romans (5:6-8):

For when we were still without strength, in due time Christ died for the ungodly. For scarcely for a righteous man will one die; yet perhaps for a good man someone would even dare to die. But God demonstrates His own love toward us, in that while we were still sinners, Christ died for us.

This is the evidence of our Creator's love for His creation. His love was not a passive sentiment but an active, sacrificial giving of Himself. He gave us His best and invited us to respond in kind, loving Him with all our hearts, minds, and strength.

God's love transcends our human comprehension. As Paul points out, it is unheard of for someone to willingly die for another, even if that person is righteous. And yet, in His boundless love, God sent His Son to die for us while we were still sinners.

This call to love God wholeheartedly is not a sign of divine desperation but an invitation to partake in His divine life. When we reject God's love, we are not subjecting ourselves to God's punishment but instead willingly stepping into the realm of death. Satan stands ready to ensnare those who spurn God's love or take it for granted.

The hymn "Souls of men why will ye scatter" poignantly reminds us of the consequences of straying from God's love.

Souls of men why will ye scatter like a crowd of frightened sheep
  Foolish hearts why will ye wander
  From a love so pure and deep

Our hearts need not wander from a love so pure and deep. God's love beckons us, calling us back to the fold and the safety and comfort of His embrace.

So, let's not scatter like frightened sheep. Let us trust in God's love, a love that was first demonstrated in creation, affirmed throughout human history, and fully revealed on the cross. It's a love that is pure and deep, a love that calls us to return and rest in God's embrace. It is the love that loved us first.

Chapter 10

Testing of Love in the Twilight of this World

"Love bears all things, believes all things, hopes all things, endures all things." - 1 Corinthians 13:7

Since the dawn of time, from creation until this very moment, we find ourselves closer to the terminus of this world than Adam ever was. The shadow of the fall of humanity looms long and deep, but God, in His infinite wisdom, set forth a divine process to raise anew a people unto Himself.

These people would inhabit a new heaven and a new earth, a testament to His divine re-creation. I am not obligated to seek your agreement on this matter, for the veracity of this truth is not tethered to mere human opinion. Instead, this truth is echoed in the words of Jesus Himself, the spiritual luminary who spoke more about heaven and eternity with God than any other individual in biblical history.

In John 14:1-3, Jesus illuminates this profound reality,

"Let not your heart be troubled; you believe in God, believe also in Me. In My Father's house are many mansions; if it were not so, I would have told you. I go to prepare a place for you. And if I go and prepare a place for you, I will come again and receive you to Myself; that where I am, there you may be also."

By His declaration, we apprehend a future, a time when the present heavens and earth will recede, yielding to the emergence of a new cosmic order. The elaboration of this divine reality is beyond the scope of this text, yet the incontrovertible truth remains - we are living in the twilight of our current world.

Jesus did not confine His discourse to the last days and the momentous events heralding His second advent. He painted a detailed tableau of human conditions and behaviors that would permeate society preceding His return and, by extension, heralding the closure of this primary world. The following passage provides a glimpse into these impending events:

Matthew 24:9-12 states,

"Then you will be handed over to be persecuted and put to death, and you will be hated by all nations because of me. At that time many will turn away from the faith and will betray and hate each other, and many false prophets will appear and deceive many people. Because of the increase of wickedness, the love of most will grow cold, but the one who stands firm to the end will be saved. And this gospel of the kingdom will be preached in the whole world as a testimony to all nations, and then the end will come."

This passage is not a mere declaration; it's a stark portrait of the conditions that would color the last days. It reflects not the physical creation but the human behaviors and interactions defining these tumultuous times.

This portrayal wields a dual-edged sword: on the one hand, it resounds with the weight of prophetic inevitability; on the other, it reverberates with the urgency of a warning meant for those with ears attuned to the whispers of the Spirit.

We find several examples in biblical history where mankind heeded divine warnings, averting potential calamity. The story of Nineveh stands as a prime example.

Consequently, the words of Jesus are not merely a prophecy set in stone; they also serve as a call to wisdom and transformation. It reminds us that, through a behavior change, we can avert being part of the prophecy's more dire implications and position ourselves to be accepted into God's kingdom.

A Stern Warning

In a world immersed in the waxing and waning of human love, the words of Jesus take on a chilling resonance. "Because iniquity abounds, the love of many will wax cold."

It is a chilling prophecy, a stern warning. When our love for God, our fellow beings, and our nations cools, it sends ripples of chaos through our existence, leading us towards a living hell on earth before the final reckoning arrives. One may introspect: Has my love for God, others, and my country, cooled down?

As we navigate these troubled waters, we witness the crumbling of moral order and the gradual erosion of conscience. Truth becomes an unwelcome stranger, justice morphs into a mockery, darkness dons the deceptive garb of light, and what was once luminous retreats into shadowy ambiguity.

The ancient standards, the moral landmarks that once guided us, are displaced as humans increasingly disregard the veracity of truth. Consequently, as Jesus forewarned, the love of many grows cold.

Apostle Paul provides a detailed sketch of this turbulent landscape that Jesus alluded to. He penned these unsettling lines to Timothy, fortifying the prophecy with his second voice of warning:

> *"But know this, that in the last days perilous times will come: For men will be lovers of themselves, lovers of money, boasters, proud, blasphemers, disobedient to parents, unthankful, unholy, unloving, unforgiving, slanderers, without self-control, brutal, despisers of good, traitors, headstrong, haughty, lovers of pleasure rather than lovers of God."* 2 Timothy 3:1-4

Paul's portrait is vivid, scarcely requiring additional illumination. One needs only to gaze upon our current world to see these prophecies made flesh.

And so, the pivotal question looms: What is the nature of your love for God in these testing times?

These are precarious times when our world has distorted the concept of light and darkness. Actions once shrouded in societal disapproval are now welcomed into the daylight without a trace of guilt.

Consider the issue of same-sex marriages and relationships for instance. It is a lifestyle that directly contradicts the commandments of God, an affront that led to the decimation of

Sodom and Gomorrah. The world has since changed its tune, declaring same-sex relationships acceptable and a right of every individual. While God hates sin, He still loves the sinner and it is His sincere desire that all will come to the saving knowledge of Jesus Christ. How then does the church of Christ position herself to effectively and efficiently play this expected role in accordance with the will of God?

Yet the Church's fracturing stance on the issue makes this shift both alarming and heartbreaking. We find church leaders and denominations divided, some even endorsing same-sex relations.

In light of these times, it is my sincere prayer that the Church will allow herself to be led by the Holy Spirit and the tenets of scripture echoing the sanctity of marriage as conceived in biblical terms: a sacred union and accompanying sexual relations exclusively between a man and a woman.

While the church may not endorse and accept these alternative lifestyles we also guided by scripture and injuncted not to kill and use violence against people we disagree with but show them the love of Christ.

Do Not Love the World

Our world, a veritable market of enticements, presents innumerable offerings that vie with the pure love believers are expected to display for God. Many struggle to rise above these siren calls.

Whether from a lack of understanding of God's Word or an attitude of nonchalant acceptance, believers are developing a palate for the world's offerings. Instead of being a beacon of light, guiding the world with our example, we find the tables reversed.

Isn't it a paradox that instead of leading the course, the Church often grapples with whether to accept or reject the world's latest introductions? This underscores the aptness and urgency of Apostle John's admonition in 1 John 2:15-17 to those who have ears to hear:

> "Do not love the world or the things in the world. If anyone loves the world, the love of the Father is not in him. For all that is in the world—the lust of the flesh, the lust of the eyes, and the pride of life—is not of the Father but is of the world. And the world is passing away, and the lust of it; but he who does the will of God abides forever."

The world unfurls before us a carpet of money, power, and fame, each with its potent charm capable of drawing the believer away from the love of God. This mirrors Satan's perpetual ploy, the same strategy that led to the Fall of Adam and Eve in the Garden of Eden.

"So when the woman saw that the tree was good for food, that it was pleasant to the eyes, and a tree desirable to make one wise, she took of its fruit and ate. She also gave to her husband with her, and he ate. Then the eyes of both of them were opened, and they knew that they were naked; and they sewed fig leaves together and made themselves coverings." Genesis 3:6-7

Just as Satan deftly packages sin, making it palatable to mankind oblivious of its dire consequences, the world seems more appealing than ever. Christians are confronted with the onerous task of discerning the death trap cloaked in allurements and evading it or succumbing to it.

In the present world, transgressions are sugar-coated with euphemisms: adultery is dubbed an 'affair,' dishonesty is commended as being 'smart,' and ruthlessness is hailed as a virtue.

We witness a generation of parents grappling to instill the principles of God's word in their children, some barely past their tenth year. The world argues for the right to self-expression, denouncing those traditional communities that insist on imparting God's commandments to their young as regressive.

The 'progressive youth,' while embracing modern notions, is adrift, uncertain of their destination. They are far from embodying the fervor of love for God, as exemplified by Joseph, Daniel, the three Hebrew young men, or Timothy. As the world descends into deeper shades of moral ambiguity, the Church is torn between pleasing the advocates of the worldly system and honoring Jehovah Almighty, whose principles remain immutable.

What does your love gravitate towards today? Are you drawn to resuming your erstwhile profession – be it a fisherman, doctor, engineer, or politician? Do these pursuits hold more charm than saving souls for the kingdom? Would you prefer to invest your riches in amassing more wealth rather than aiding ministries dedicated to serving humanity?

The Church today is confronting the real test of our love for God. While our words have repeatedly reverberated across the globe, amplified by social media, are we genuinely embodying the principles we preach?

From the world's perspective, the Church appears to be

losing its seriousness as it competes for the same worldly pleasures it preaches against. Instead of standing out as a beacon of God's love, we seek Scriptural justifications for embracing the world's allurements.

However, it's not the reach of our voices that matter to God, but our lifestyle and our response to the test of love in these challenging times.

Chapter 11

Return to your First Love

"He said 'Love...as I have loved you.' We cannot love too much." - Amy Carmichael

A walk down memory lane, peering into the origin of our relationships, often yields recollections of love, fervor, and a relentless pursuit of commitment. It's a common tactic counselors employ to rekindle the embers of dying love in a strained relationship.

The individuals involved are often asked, "How did it all begin? What were the things that brought you together that ignited your love, which now seems to be under the ashes?"

To highlight the Christian's predicament, I turn to countless stories of couples who stood against all odds to unite with their chosen life partners. They faced the opposition of family, friends, and society, yet stood their ground because of a profound love for each other.

In the face of adversity, they uttered statements such as "I truly love him" or "I truly love her," affirming that their love could overpower any opposition.

There is an uncanny parallel between this passionate love between couples and the love we should have for Christ, as stated in Matthew 10:37, *"Anyone who loves their father or mother more than me is not worthy of me; anyone who loves their son or daughter more than me is not worthy of me."*

In the throes of their love, couples often question, "Do you love your parents more than me?" If the answer is no, they forge ahead and unite in marriage. But it is heartbreaking that, years later, the same love wanes, and couples seek separation.

The Christian journey mirrors this marital scenario. Christ beckons us, just like the counselor, to revisit the origin of our relationship with Him, to rekindle that first love. The Church of Ephesus, described in Revelation 2:1-7, is a classic example. The Scripture reads,

> *"To the angel of the church in Ephesus write: 'The words of him who holds the seven stars in his right hand, who walks among the seven golden lampstands. 'I know your works, your toil and your patient endurance, and how you cannot bear with those who are evil, but have tested those who call themselves apostles and are not, and found them to be false. I know you are enduring patiently and bearing up for my name's sake, and you have not grown weary. But I have this against you, that you have abandoned the love you had at first. Remember therefore from where you have fallen; repent, and do the works you did at first. If not, I will come to you and remove your lampstand from its place, unless you repent."*

While the Ephesian Church was commended for their deeds, toil, and perseverance, God reproached them for losing their first love. He urged them to remember, repent, and return to the works they did at the beginning. This message resonates with us, the present-day Church, who, in the journey of faith, may have strayed from our first love for God.

Reflecting on our personal walk with God, we realize that we've strayed from our initial fervor for the things of God. At the inception of our Christian journey, we experienced an intense flame of passion for God and His Kingdom.

Sin became repulsive; we developed a zeal for holiness and a passion for lost souls. We became unstoppable missionaries, leveraging every platform—buses, taxis, beaches—to proclaim the gospel. We even offered our resources and services to the Church without expecting any compensation.

As time passed, however, that blazing fire seemed to have dwindled. Our passion for God's work has cooled down, replaced by excuses and complaints. Some argue that the changes in our lives and society have necessitated this shift. While it is true that times have changed, we must ponder upon what has truly changed. Is it, not our love for God that has dwindled?

In the past, when phones were a rarity, believers walked miles to fellowship with brethren and share the gospel. Today, with the conveniences of modern technology, cars, and telecommunication devices, how have we utilized these resources for the gospel? Have they drawn us closer to God or distanced us from our first love?

> *"And to the angel of the church of the Laodiceans write, 'These things says the Amen, the Faithful and True Witness, the Beginning of the creation of God:* [1]*"I know your works, that you are neither cold nor hot. I could wish you were cold or hot. So then, because you are lukewarm, and neither cold nor hot, I will vomit you out of My mouth. Because you say, 'I am rich, have become wealthy, and have need of nothing'—and do not know that you are wretched, miserable, poor, blind, and naked.* Revelation 3:14-16

The church in Laodicea received a stern warning from God in Revelation 3:14-16 because they were neither cold nor hot, but lukewarm. Their inconsistency and unsteady behavior earned them a severe rebuke. They lived a double life, oscillating between worldly pleasures and their Christian faith. God warned that such a lifestyle is repugnant to Him and demanded total allegiance.

Elijah confronted the Israelites in a similar situation on Mount Carmel in 1 Kings 18:20-21, challenging them to make a clear choice:

> *So Ahab sent for all the children of Israel, and gathered the prophets together on Mount Carmel. And Elijah came to all the people, and said, "How long will you falter between two opinions? If the Lord is God, follow Him; but if Baal, follow him." But the people answered him not a word.*

The story ended tragically for some as they faced the consequences of their indecision.

God's desire, however, is not to punish us but to call us back to our first love. He desires us to bask in His love, follow Him wholeheartedly, and in doing so, experience the richness of His blessings.

We do not do God any favor by loving Him; instead, we are the beneficiaries of His abundant grace and mercy. The call to return to our first love is to experience a renewed, fervent love for God, one that overcomes every trial and test. As we return to our first love, let us remember the fervor of our early faith and rekindle it, lighting the way for others in the journey of faith.

The Story of Mark

Consider Mark's story to better illustrate what it means to return to your first love.

Mark grew up in a religious family where church attendance was more of a ritual than a relationship with God. However, upon encountering a vibrant Christian fellowship during his college years, Mark experienced a spiritual rebirth.

He vividly remembers that period of his life as a season of intense love for God and passion for the things of the Kingdom. Sin became repugnant to him; he had a hunger for righteousness and a burning desire to reach out to the lost. Every conversation was an opportunity for him to share the gospel. He volunteered tirelessly in his church, even using the little resources he had to give to the church and the furtherance of the Gospel.

But as Mark progressed in life, things began to change. Upon graduation, he landed a lucrative job that consumed much of his time and energy. With an increased income, he could now afford a car and a smartphone, which, while convenient, also served as distractions. The digital world drew him in, with social media, news, and entertainment competing for his time and attention.

Sunday services became an obligation rather than a joyous fellowship, and his involvement in church activities dwindled. His car was often used for pleasure trips rather than gospel outreaches, and his phone became a tool for endless scrolling rather than bible reading or sharing Christian content. His fervor for God was replaced by a love for comfort and convenience.

One day, as he sat in a Sunday service, the pastor read from the book of Revelation about the Church of Ephesus. It was as if a mirror was held before Mark. He realized he had lost his first love for God. He reflected on his initial days of being born again, how he was zealous for God, how sin looked so dark, and how he fervently spread the gospel. He asked himself, "What happened to that fire?"

Like the Church of Ephesus, Mark realized he needed to remember his first love, repent, and do the things he did at first. He realized he needed to use his blessings – his job, car, smartphone – not as distractions but as tools to serve God and spread His word. He needed to shift his priorities and rekindle the fire he once had for God.

Mark's life serves as a poignant reminder for us to examine our own lives. Have we, like Mark, lost our first love for God? Have the blessings and conveniences of life distracted us from our primary love for God and His Kingdom? It is time for us to return to our first love, to rekindle our passion for God, and to utilize our resources for His glory.

Chapter 12

Acts of Love for God

"Love is not patronizing and charity isn't about pity, it is about love. Charity and love are the same -- with charity you give love, so don't just give money but reach out your hand (too)." - Mother Teresa

Just as our spoken words of love require credible evidence, so does our proclamation of love for God demand tangible proof. After all, isn't it often said that "actions speak louder than words"?

As we navigate through this chapter, we shall explore how acts of love towards God, exemplified by several figures from the Old Testament, transcend the verbal declarations often found in religious gatherings.

Imagine yourself as a fly on the wall in a couples counseling session. A woman sits on the sofa, wringing her hands and casting nervous glances at her husband. "He doesn't love me," she insists. The husband retorts, visibly upset, "I don't understand why she thinks that. She knows I love her."

What follows is a familiar dance of accusations and justifications. She details unmet expectations and gestures unmade; he lists actions to prove his affection. Their narratives show how their cultural and societal backgrounds have shaped their perceptions of love.

Their love languages differ, creating a chasm of misunderstanding. The exchange clearly demonstrates that love, while universally craved, needs to be expressed in ways that resonate with the recipient.

John the Apostle, in his epistle, brings this truth into sharp focus:

> *"My little children, let us not love in word or in tongue, but in deed and in truth. And by this we know that we are of the truth, and shall assure our hearts before Him. For if our heart condemns us, God is greater than our heart, and knows all things."* - 1 John 3:18-20

John asserts that love must manifest through actions – a form of 'deeds' that transcend mere verbal declarations. When words seem hollow, deeds become the vessel for love, reaching to touch the beloved's heart.

In critical times, these deeds, aligned with truth and sincerity, delineate our spiritual positioning. They are our responses to the litmus test of faith when faced with societal greed and self-absorption.

So, what does it mean to love God? How do we express this love tangibly?

As we delve into the lives of specific individuals from the Bible, we learn practical ways they demonstrated their love for God. From Abraham's radical obedience to David's devout worship, we find models of action-oriented love.

These figures give us a roadmap for a love that transcends lip service – a love that is substantial, transformative, and utterly devoted to God. As we tread this path, we discover that loving God authentically and thoroughly is a compass that never leads us astray.

In this chapter, we will examine a few biblical figures, understand their acts of love for God, and draw lessons that can guide us in our journey of faith. As we emulate their devotion, may our lives become love letters to God, written not with ink but with acts of faith, hope, and love.

David's Affection for the Lord

We are bestowed with the unique privilege of learning from the man after God's own heart - King David. This affection for God manifests in countless ways throughout his reign. We find an enlightening example in 1 Chronicles 29, where David speaks to the assembly about the preparation for building God's temple:

> *"Furthermore, King David said to all the assembly: 'My son Solomon, whom alone God has chosen, is young and inexperienced; and the work is great because the temple is not for man but for the LORD God. Now for the house of my God, I have prepared with all my might: gold for things to be made of gold, silver for things of silver, bronze for things of bronze, iron for*

things of iron, wood for things of wood, onyx stones, stones to be set, glistening stones of various colors, all kinds of precious stones, and marble slabs in abundance. Moreover, because I have set my affection on the house of my God, I have given to the house of my God, over and above all that I have prepared for the holy house, my own special treasure of gold and silver...' " 1 Chronicles 29:1-5

Examine the lengths David went to in preparing for the temple's construction. His offerings went far beyond what was initially planned. But what's even more remarkable than the king's extraordinary gifts are the motives that guided him.

David's grand preparations for the temple were fueled by his profound love for the Lord. He affirms this by saying that he had set his affection on the house of God.

When a person claims to have set their affection on something, it suggests an unwavering commitment, a willingness to go to any lengths for the well-being of that cherished entity.

Just as a man deeply in love with a woman might shower her with lavish gifts, emptying his coffers to express his affection, so did David's love for God compel him to give generously. But our narrative here transcends the earthly realm of romantic love, exploring the deep spiritual affection of King David for God and His works.

A verse from an old hymn declares, "You can't outgive God, no matter how you try." It's unlikely David was attempting to outdo God in his offerings, but the motivation behind his extravagant giving caught God's attention and pleased Him.

David's offerings for the sanctity of God's house were not born out of sympathy or manipulation but were a testament to his deep love for God. It's crucial to remember that God never overlooks acts of love towards Him from His creations, especially from His highest creation – humans.

Such expressions of affection are like a sweet-smelling aroma, a heavenly perfume that fills the corridors of heaven, drawing God's undivided attention to the giver.

This affectionate and generous love set David apart from all other kings of Israel. It prompts us to ask, can it be said of us that we, too, have set our affection on the things God cherishes?

After all, God cares deeply about His Church, the souls within it, and all of humanity. Like David, may our love for God inspire us to go beyond the expected, to commit ourselves entirely to the things God holds dear, and in doing so, walk in the footsteps of a man after God's own heart.

Solomon's Love for the Lord

Let us now turn our attention to another pivotal character in the narrative of God's love, Solomon, the son of David. He stands as a compelling testament to the power of parental guidance, demonstrating how profoundly a father's love for God can influence his child's spiritual path.

> *"And Solomon loved the LORD, walking in the statutes of his father David, except that he sacrificed and burned incense at the high places. Now the king went to Gibeon to sacrifice there, for that was the great high place: Solomon offered a thousand burnt offerings on that altar. At Gibeon, the LORD appeared to Solomon in a dream by night; and God said, "Ask! What shall I give you?"* 1 Kings 3:3-5

Of all the children of David, Solomon stands out in his love for the Lord. Unlike his brothers, Adonijah and Absalom, Solomon's life bore the distinct imprint of his father's spiritual legacy. The love Solomon had for God was not spontaneous or incidental. It was the fruit of what he observed in David, his father, who taught him how to love the Lord.

This instruction from a father to his son offers a potent reminder to all parents. We have a divine obligation to our children, not just to express our love for the Lord in words but to demonstrate and prove it through our actions. It is these lived experiences of faith, these tangible demonstrations of God's love, that will guide our children on their spiritual journey.

Do you recall that significant night when God stepped into Solomon's life and offered him a blank check of blessings? Solomon's act of offering a thousand burnt offerings was indeed significant.

But what indeed lent its value, what truly stirred the heart of God, was the underlying motivation of love. Solomon's love for God was so profound that it reached the heavens and moved God to bless him beyond measure. As the narrative unfolds, Solomon becomes the wisest and wealthiest king of his era, an accolade confirmed when the Queen of Sheba herself was astounded by Solomon's unprecedented wisdom and wealth.

In these critical times, when the world teeters on the brink of monumental spiritual change, the act of giving to support God's work assumes unparalleled importance. The fields are ripe for harvest, yet the laborers are few.

There is an urgent need for missionary programs around the globe and church buildings to nurture the souls won through evangelism. As the custodians of God's love, what are we doing to make these happen?

In the same way that David's example guided Solomon, let our acts of love for God echo down the generations, inspiring our children and grandchildren to build a world that radiates God's love. Let our love for God be so evident and authentic that it becomes a beacon for others, just as Solomon's love became a beacon for the generations that followed.

Hezekiah's Unswerving Love for God

Let us journey once more into the annals of the Old Testament, revisiting the remarkable story of Hezekiah, the King of Judah. His life is a testament to the assertion that God acknowledges our love for Him and rewards it richly.

> *"In those days Hezekiah was sick and near death. And Isaiah the prophet, the son of Amoz, went to him and said to him, 'Thus says the LORD: 'Set your house in order, for you shall die, and not live."' Then he turned his face toward the wall, and prayed to the LORD, saying, 'Remember now, O LORD, I pray, how I have walked before You in truth and with a loyal heart, and have done what was good in Your sight.' And Hezekiah wept bitterly. And it happened, before Isaiah had gone out into the middle court, that the word of the LORD came to him, saying, 'Return and tell Hezekiah the leader of My people, 'Thus says the LORD, the God of David your father: 'I have heard your prayer, I have seen your tears; surely I will heal you.'" 2 Kings 20:1-5*

Unravel the narrative thread by thread, if you will. In God's ineffable wisdom, He sent His servant, the prophet Isaiah, to convey a dire message to Hezekiah: death was looming near. No reason was assigned, and we should not seek one, for it was the expression of God's sovereign will.

Faced with this grim prospect, Hezekiah did not despair. Instead, he turned his face towards the wall and presented his plea to the Lord. In his supplication, Hezekiah pointed to his unwavering fidelity to God's commandments and his efforts to serve Him faithfully.

And lo and behold, God heard his plea. He did more than just hear; He empathized with Hezekiah's grief, understood his anguish, and decided to grant him a life extension. It seemed as if God was moved by Hezekiah's fidelity, asserting that a man of such love and loyalty deserved to enjoy a few more sunrises.

Hezekiah's story teaches us a profound lesson. When genuine and enduring, our love for God elevates our worth in His eyes. And when God acknowledges this value, He rewards us generously.

Just as Hezekiah's life of love and loyalty prompted God to extend his days, so too can our steadfast love for God bring forth blessings. God, in His infinite faithfulness, recognizes, cherishes, and rewards the love we bear for Him.

In our journeys of faith, let Hezekiah's story inspire us. No matter the adversities we encounter, may we love God unwaveringly, walk in His truth faithfully, and serve Him loyally, confident in the knowledge that our love for Him has inestimable value in His divine eyes.

Chapter 13

Acts of Love in the New Testament

"God bestows His blessings without discrimination. The followers of Jesus are children of God, and they should manifest the family likeness by doing good to all, even to those who deserve the opposite." - F. F. Bruce

As we delve further into Acts of Love for God, our focus shifts towards narratives rooted in the New Testament and explores how these timeless lessons may guide the church today in showcasing our love for God.

Our exploration commences with the notion of commitment to the Body of Christ. A deep love for God often manifests as a consistent engagement with His people.

The question then arises: To what extent are we willing to endure in demonstrating love for God? And where does our first love reside?

Many abandon the church for a myriad of reasons, constructing rationales to justify their departure, all the while disregarding that love for God is intricately woven into the fabric of loving His people. Abstaining from the church merely because of a discordant note or a perceived slight is not emblematic of God's love.

There are those for whom the slightest rainfall serves as a sufficient deterrent from attending church as if they are actively seeking an excuse to forsake fellowship. Ironically, such individuals would brave the rain, armed with raincoats and umbrellas, to catch a flight or attend an important societal function.

Yet, I have also witnessed an entirely different demeanor. I refer to individuals who radiate an intense love for God that transcends commonplace inconveniences.

Consider the case of a church member who ventured out to deliver his tithe despite being weighed down by a heavy cold and fever. His sickness was of the nature that mandated isolation, primarily to prevent its spread. Regardless, this faithful believer drove to the Church, submitted his tithe enveloped, and promptly returned home to convalesce. His rationale? "This belongs to God, and I cannot keep it with me." Such an act can only be fueled by love for God.

In another instance, a woman was due to embark on an extended trip. Before her departure, she arrived at the church to drop off her tithes. These stories underscore individuals who maintain a consciousness of God and harbor an unflinching love for Him and His affairs.

They recognize that their possessions are, in fact, gifts from God, and they must return to Him what is due, irrespective of their circumstances.

These acts of love, underpinned by faith and commitment, do not go unnoticed in the eyes of the Lord. Indeed, God acknowledges such dedication and invariably rewards His faithful, loving followers. So, let these stories inspire us to consider how we can demonstrate our love for God in our daily lives and remind us that such acts of love never go unnoticed.

Engaging in the Father's Business

When Jesus, merely twelve years old, told his bewildered parents, "I must be about my Father's business," he planted a spiritual seed for all of us to nourish and cultivate.

The idea is that nothing should supersede God's business in our lives—not our efforts to secure financial stability, not our dreams of prestigious schools for our children or million-dollar homes, not even our personal ambitions, including those pursued in the name of the gospel. The heart of God's business beats for winning souls and preparing them for Heaven.

If we truly abide by this divine mandate, our world today will witness much more of the transformative power of God. Consider the funds we amass for the ministry. How much is directly funneled into nourishing the spiritual growth of God's people?

For the entrepreneurs among us, what percentage of our profits supports the establishment of new churches, aiding the nurturing and discipleship of newly won souls?

While it's essential to attend to our earthly duties, let us remember the true purpose of our existence: to be preoccupied with our Father's business. The final judgment will not pivot on our professional accomplishments but on whether we have fulfilled our divine mandate. God's expectation is clear: we are to be immersed in His work.

Every engagement in this life offers us an opportunity to serve God, whether through serving our country, upholding justice as a lawyer, preserving health as a doctor, or spreading good news as a journalist or media professional. We are all called to be ambassadors for God, perpetually engrossed in His affairs.

Yet, there are twelve-year-olds today who, unlike Jesus, are mired in confusion. Some university students, well past their seventeenth year, are still grappling to comprehend life's purpose. The most remarkable breakthrough in life occurs when you unearth the purpose for which you were created and discern that unique duty assigned to you alone. By this measure, we will be assessed as we transition into eternity.

Eternity presents itself in two forms: with or without Jesus. The nature of our eternal existence is intimately tied to how we navigate our earthly lives. How are we deploying our resources, talents, and time? Are they directed toward the Father's business or consumed for personal gain? This question demands our sincere reflection, for it is our acts of love for God that will shape the contours of our eternal destiny.

The Love of a Non-Jew

In the expansive tapestry of New Testament events, one particular incident stands out vividly, illustrating the power of love for God's kingdom. This story, wonderfully narrated in Luke 7:4-5, revolves around an unlikely protagonist: a non-Jew, a Roman Centurion.

"Now when He concluded all His sayings in the hearing of the people, He entered Capernaum. And a certain centurion's servant, who was dear to him, was sick and ready to die. So when he heard about Jesus, he sent elders of the Jews to Him, pleading with Him to come and heal his servant. And when they came to Jesus, they begged Him earnestly, saying that the one for whom He should do this was deserving, 'for he loves our nation, and has built us a synagogue.'"

What makes this account particularly striking is the man's Roman soldier status and his desperate need for Jesus's divine intervention. The Jewish elders approached Jesus on his behalf. Their testimony shed light on the centurion's righteousness, declaring him worthy of Jesus's healing touch.

But why would they vouch for a Roman, a foreigner in their land? The answer lay in his actions. He harbored a profound love for the Jewish nation, and this love manifested in the synagogue he built for the Jewish people. Jesus, acknowledging this act of love, granted the centurion's request.

Love for God's people and their worship made this non-Jew a worthy recipient of divine mercy. His act of constructing a place of worship revealed a genuine affection for the nation of Israel and, by extension, God Himself. It's a powerful testament to the eternal rewards that await those who express their love for God by building places of worship for His people today.

So, pause for a moment. Reflect deeply and ask yourself the compelling question: "What is my level of care for God and His kingdom?" This self-interrogation will guide you in expressing genuine love for God, reaping eternal rewards, and making your mark in Heaven's annals.

Jesus Questions Peter's Love

Dusk had fallen, and the glow of a new day had risen when a profoundly significant interaction took place on the shores of the Sea of Galilee. Breaking bread together, a hushed, earnest conversation ensued between Jesus and Simon Peter, his steadfast disciple. Embedded within this dialogue is a profoundly moving and eternally relevant question: "Simon, son of Jonah, do you love me more than these?"

Like a refrain in a haunting melody, Jesus poses this question to Peter three times, his gaze steady, his tone filled with tenderness. Each time, Peter responds affirmatively, his words underscored by a sincerity that perhaps even he hadn't fully recognized until that moment.

Yet each affirmation of love is met with a divine commission: "Feed my lambs," "Tend my sheep," "Feed my sheep."

In the echo of Peter's proclamation of love, we hear Jesus' mandate for our lives. The call to feed His sheep is an invitation to the profound privilege of participating in His kingdom's work - to care for those He cherishes deeply. But it is more than an invitation; it is an expectation intrinsically tied to our love for Him.

There is an inextricable link between our love for Christ and our care for His people. It's a love that looks beyond ourselves, our needs, desires, and comforts. It is a love that propels us into action, calling us to sacrifice, serve, and shepherd. The heart of Jesus yearns for His flock with a love that led Him to the cross, a love that triumphed over death itself.

As His followers, we are called to love His flock with the

same depth, fervor, and selfless devotion. As Jesus entrusted Peter with this sacred responsibility, He also entrusts us.

Whether we are pastors, teachers, parents, or simply disciples seeking to follow in Christ's footsteps, we each have a role in nurturing His flock. Are we embracing this mandate with the understanding that it is not merely a duty but a profound act of love for our Savior?

Loving Your Neighbor

A sliver of moonlight spilled over the gathering of Pharisees as one amongst them, a lawyer, strode forth with a challenge posed to the Man who dared speak truths that ruffled their long-held beliefs.

"Teacher," he began, his voice echoing in the quiet night air, "which is the great commandment in the law?" What unfolded next, as recorded in the Gospel of Matthew, reveals the heart of God's law: love.

The answer Jesus offered was simple yet revolutionary. He first echoed the age-old commandment from Deuteronomy, "You shall love the LORD your God with all your heart, with all your soul, and with all your mind," affirming that loving God is indeed the greatest commandment.

But then, in the same breath, He extended this profound law of love to include our neighbors. He declared, "And the second is like it: 'You shall love your neighbor as yourself.'"

This pairing of love for God and love for neighbor was not a careless juxtaposition. It was a deliberate unveiling of God's expectation that our love for Him must be tangibly expressed in our love for our fellow man.

This is a truth that the apostle John underlined powerfully in his first epistle, "If someone says, 'I love God,' and hates his brother, he is a liar; for he who does not love his brother whom he has seen, how can he love God whom he has not seen?"

John's words stir us with their stark simplicity. They invite us to examine our hearts, to confront the dissonance between our professions of love for God and our attitudes towards those who bear His image, our neighbors.

It is, indeed, a simple yet profound logic: if we claim to love God, whom we do not see, how can we not extend the same love to those whom we see daily, to those who bear His image and likeness?

Sadly, it is often the ones we worship alongside, our brothers and sisters in faith, whom we fail to love as we ought. We might stand shoulder to shoulder with them in church, singing songs of love to God while harboring resentment or bitterness in our hearts towards them.

And yet, we expect God to receive our offerings and tithes as expressions of our love for Him, forgetting that these offerings are collected by the hands of our fellow men and women, the visible representatives of God.

The teachings of Jesus remind us that our acts of love toward God cannot be separated from our acts of love toward our fellow human beings. In seeing, respecting, and loving God's image in others, we truly express our love for Him. Regardless of one's background, status, or beliefs, every person carries the divine image, and in loving them, we love God.

Love Your Enemies

Walking deeper into the labyrinth of divine love, we encounter an even more radical teaching of Christ. It is a teaching that challenges the very core of our human tendencies and conventional wisdom: love your enemies.

The narrative is imbued in Matthew 5:43-45, where Jesus instructs us to transcend the ordinary to attain the extraordinary: to be as perfect as our Heavenly Father. The One who loves indiscriminately, even those who rise against Him daily.

The common sentiment of loving our allies and harboring animosity against our adversaries stands dismantled in the Kingdom of God. Such dichotomy is obsolete in the sacred landscape of love. There is no room for it within hearts that have been sanctified by the sacrificial blood of Christ.

We are redeemed, forgiven, justified, and lovingly accepted into the divine family. Therefore, our love must mirror that of the Father—embracing all humanity, regardless of their deeds, for they too are beneficiaries of the holy work carried out on Calvary.

Jesus's injunction, 'love your enemies,' not only contradicts human instincts but also elevates us to the heights of divine love. It casts us apart as the genuine children of God, distinguishing us from the rest of the world. Jesus declares in Matthew 5:44,

> "But I say to you, love your enemies, bless those who curse you, do good to those who hate you, and pray for those who spitefully use you and persecute you, that you may be sons of your Father

in heaven; for He makes His sun rise on the evil and on the good, and sends rain on the just and on the unjust."

The parable of the Good Samaritan in Luke 10:31-34 casts a powerful spotlight on this profound teaching.

Now by chance a certain priest came down that road. And when he saw him, he passed by on the other side. Likewise a Levite, when he arrived at the place, came and looked, and passed by on the other side. But a certain Samaritan, as he journeyed, came where he was. And when he saw him, he had compassion. So he went to him and bandaged his wounds, pouring on oil and wine; and he set him on his own animal, brought him to an inn, and took care of him.

A priest and a Levite, two men revered in Jewish society and undoubtedly, proclaimers of their love for God, cross paths with a suffering man. Yet, they choose to bypass him. They rush towards their synagogue, their sanctuary of worship, forsaking the living testament of their love for God lying by the wayside.

The man was a Samaritan, an outsider in their eyes, unworthy of their care and compassion. They rush to show their love for the unseen God yet ignore His visible creation.

However, it is a Samaritan, despised by the Jews, who becomes the beacon of God's love. On his journey, he stumbles upon the wounded man and, filled with compassion, tends to his wounds, embodies the spirit of the divine command, and does unto others what he would have wanted to be done unto him.

In their neglect and compassion, Jesus unveils the paradox

of divine love. He uncovers the profound challenge at the heart of His teachings: to see each individual, irrespective of their identity or deeds, as the beloved child of God. To love them as we love ourselves and to love God. Only then can we truly heed the call to love our enemies and mirror our Heavenly Father's boundless, all-embracing love.

Richard Wurmbrand - Tortured for Christ

Let me share a story narrated by Richard Wurmbrand, a Christian missionary who underwent relentless torture for his faith in Christ within the boundaries of the former Soviet Republic.

Wurmbrand recounts the story of two Chinese Christians huddled in a cold prison cell. Each clung to a thin blanket for warmth, battling the chilling sting of the bitter cold. One of the Christians, noticing his brother's trembling figure, was gripped by a compelling thought: "If that were Christ, would you give Him your blanket?"

Without hesitation, the answer resonated in his heart, "Of course, I would." And so, he cast his blanket over his brother, quelling his shivers with warmth. This act underlined a profound truth – he could not proclaim his love for Jesus, whom he could not see while disregarding the visible suffering of his brother.

This touching account highlights one of the most significant challenges confronting Christians today: the actualization of love in our daily lives. Our affection for God must not only be perfect but also extend to all those who surround us. It is an ideal that often eludes the church in our current times, causing our expressions of love to be reduced to mere verbal affirmations.

The command we have received is unambiguous: we are to love God, who is unseen, and our neighbors, who are in plain sight. Each of us has a unique opportunity to assess our adherence to this commandment and engage in a sincere dialogue with God, who alone can guide us to become His perfect children.

To deepen our understanding and practice of love, here are some steps for introspection and spiritual growth:

Begin each day with a prayer asking God to reveal the profundity of His love for you. Reflect upon your life before accepting Christ and envisage your existence's trajectory without His divine intervention. Allow the consciousness of Jesus' love for you to pervade your being each morning.

Contemplate the transformation that God's love has wrought within you. He did not merely liberate you from the clutches of darkness but ushered you into His radiant light, granting you a rejuvenated existence. Recall your previous anonymity, now replaced by a recognition that stems from God's love.

Periodically examine the actions you have undertaken out of love for God. Distinguish between the deeds intended to gratify your ego or gain approval from others and those genuinely motivated by your love for God.

Pray for the Holy Spirit to illuminate your heart, dispelling all remnants of darkness, so your heart can remain pure and pliant, making it easier for you to love God.

Pray for the grace to see Christ in every believer with whom you share your worship. When you sit beside a fellow believer, ponder: "If this were Christ, how would I express my love for Him? What gestures of love does this person deserve from me?"

Ask God to expand your capacity to love, especially those you perceive as antagonistic towards you. Remember, the divine image resides in every person, including the derided drunkard next door. This image warrants your love if your devotion to God is genuine.

Let us remind ourselves that love, as described in the Bible, transcends mere emotions. It demands action, sacrifice, and the ability to see God in every face we encounter. It is a journey towards achieving the divine perfection exemplified by our Heavenly Father.

Pass the Test

We exist in an era where our love for God is relentlessly tested. Often, it is not through the dramatic trials that Job or the early saints faced but through subtle, mundane situations that we may all too easily overlook.

As a result, we risk inadvertently failing these tests, repeatedly missing out on countless opportunities to express our love for God. Such is the predicament that might provoke God to ask us, "Do you really love me?"

In the face of such a profound inquiry, we might find ourselves unsettled, even staggered. But let us not falter or despair. Instead, let us pray for increased sensitivity to the divine nudges of the Holy Spirit, guiding us to recognize these tests when they present themselves. Let us pray for a greater awareness of the people around us, the trials they face, and the opportunities they represent for us to embody God's love.

In this journey of faith, every interaction we have, and every decision we make, can serve as an expression of our love for God. As we look inward and reflect on our actions, let us strive to discern these opportunities and respond with genuine love, following the teachings of Christ.

In conclusion of this chapter, the ability to love God, our neighbors, and even our enemies is not an unattainable ideal. Instead, it is an everyday practice, a lifelong journey, a divine mandate deeply woven into our very existence as followers of Christ.

This love is not simply a feeling, but a transformative force that guides our actions, shapes our relationships, and deepens our connection with the Divine. It is the profound truth that every encounter, every person, presents an opportunity to love, serve, and reflect God's boundless, all-encompassing love into the world.

May we embrace this love with open hearts, open minds, and open arms, ever striving to fulfill the greatest commandment bestowed upon us: to love God with all our heart, soul, and mind and our neighbors as ourselves.

Chapter 14

Love for All People

"God's love is meteoric, his loyalty astronomic, His purpose titanic, his verdicts oceanic. Yet in his largeness nothing gets lost; Not a man, not a mouse, slips through the cracks." - Psalm 36:5-6, The Message (Eugene H. Peterson)

The threads of love that have been meticulously woven through the preceding chapters of this book have primarily centered around our love for God and the Body of Christ. In this chapter, however, we shift our focus from the vertical axis of our love for God and the Body of Christ to the horizontal plane of our relationships with our fellow human beings.

The insight shared here does not discriminate; it envelops all individuals, regardless of faith, social standing, circumstance, or ethnicity. It implores us to radiate God's love towards a non-believing world, extending to them a lifeline of divine affection, hoping to welcome them into the Kingdom of God.

And in a similar vein, we are to extend this love to our brethren, fostering familial bonds and unity. After all, Jesus said that our love for one another would be a marker of our discipleship.

Love: The Greatest of All

The Apostle Paul, in his epistle to the church in Corinth, pens perhaps the most profound treatise on the nature of love.

> *"Though I speak with the tongues of men and of angels, but have not love, I have become sounding brass or a clanging cymbal. And though I have the gift of prophecy, and understand all mysteries and all knowledge, and though I have all faith, so that I could remove mountains, but have not love, I am nothing. And though I bestow all my goods to feed the poor, and though I give my body to be burned, but have not love, it profits me nothing."* 1 Corinthians 13:1-3

In this heartfelt message, Paul underscores the futility of even the most formidable gifts, knowledge, and acts of faith if they are devoid of love. Bereft of love, our spiritual prowess is reduced to mere "noisome oblivion," a clanging cymbal in an empty hall echoing into nothingness. He continues:

> *"Love suffers long and is kind; love does not envy; love does not parade itself, is not puffed up; does not behave rudely, does not seek its own, is not provoked, thinks no evil; does not rejoice in iniquity, but rejoices in the truth; bears all things, believes all things, hopes all things, endures all things."*

The word 'charity' that appears in some passage translations is derived from the Greek word 'Agape,' which signifies love, affection, goodwill, and benevolence. The true nature of our love becomes evident when it is tested against these qualities.

As we venture forth in our faith journey, remember to root all our actions, thoughts, and relationships in love. As Paul so eloquently states, even the grandest of our spiritual gifts are naught if they are not underpinned by love.

Longsuffering: The First Fruit of Love

The inaugural trait of love is longsuffering. The Greek term, 'makrothymein,' predominantly used in the New Testament, is always applied to patience with people, not circumstances. It represents patience, endurance, constancy, perseverance, forbearance, and a slow pace in avenging wrongs.

It is about:

- A patience that doesn't just tolerate but forbears.
- When provoked, the ability to exercise sound judgment and restraint, opting for patience rather than an instinctive, retaliatory response.
- Dealing with others the way God deals with us - patiently, giving us ample room to grow, mature, and change our ways, rather than seeking immediate revenge.
- Tolerance of others' shortcomings and the ability to rise above others' wrongs.
- Accepting people despite how difficult, offensive, or hurtful they may be.

Longsuffering, as Modeled by King David

When King David had the chance to kill King Saul in the cave, his love for God and his desire to please Him led him to demonstrate 'makrothymein' - longsuffering, even when he had the power to harm Saul.

To the world and his men, it seemed like the logical action, a golden opportunity divinely given to end his plight. However, with a deep understanding of God's ways and precepts, David restrained himself. He even repented for merely cutting a piece of Saul's garment.

David's patience was extraordinary. Despite numerous attempts on his life by Saul, David never retaliated. He patiently weathered it all, even grieving Saul's death. This embodies the essence of 'Makrothymein' - a long patience, endurance, and forbearance in dealing with people, keeping our eyes on people rather than circumstances.

David's patience was tested in that cave. However, his love for God and respect for His commands governed his actions, preventing him from seizing the seemingly tempting opportunity to kill Saul. By showing restraint, David avoided a cycle of violence that could have haunted his reign.

This testing of longsuffering and patience when dealing with others is a measure of love. When others wrong you, and you hold the power to retaliate, choosing instead to curb your anger and display forbearance, you are embodying a Godly love. The Bible recounts this divine patience numerous times:

Psalms 103:8 states, *"The LORD is merciful and gracious, slow to anger, and plenteous in mercy."*

In Exodus 34:6, we find, *"The LORD, The LORD God,*

merciful and gracious, longsuffering, and abundant in goodness and truth."

And again in Nehemiah 9:17, *"but thou art a God ready to pardon, gracious and merciful, slow to anger, and of great kindness, and forsookest them not."* God's love is tolerant, lenient, and understanding. It is slow to anger, exercises self-restraint, and demonstrates self-control.

James 1:19 says, *"Wherefore, my beloved brethren, let every man be swift to hear, slow to speak, slow to wrath."*

Proverbs 25:28 further states, *"He that hath no rule over his own spirit is like a city that is broken down, and without walls."* A person who lacks self-control is vulnerable and susceptible to attack.

Will you put God first when tested? Can you bear long with people in the face of adversity? Will you uphold the mandate to endure long suffering out of your love for God and humanity?

Ephesians 4:1-3 exhorts us:

"I, therefore, the prisoner of the Lord, beseech you to walk worthy of the calling with which you were called, with all lowliness and gentleness, with longsuffering, bearing with one another in love, endeavoring to keep the unity of the Spirit in the bond of peace."

As we journey towards embodying this longsuffering, we draw closer to the heart of God's love, living out our calling with grace and patience.

Kindness

Kindness is a divine echo reverberating from love's tender heart, more than forgiving an offender or showing them goodness. It encompasses a deep concern for the well-being of others, expressing compassion, exceeding mere justice, and stepping into the realm of grace.

Those who have offended must acknowledge their transgressions, even if only to themselves. This is a crucial step towards repentance and a heart's transformation.

The Life of Joseph: A Testament of Kindness

Joseph's life presents a vivid portrait of kindness in action. In Genesis 45, we see Joseph not merely forgiving his brothers but going to great lengths to show them kindness even after they had wronged him.

In Genesis 45:4, Joseph beckons his brothers to "come near," embracing those who had harmed him. Most people instinctively want to distance themselves from their offenders. But the actual test of love lies in our ability to invite closeness, even when we could have sought revenge. Joseph goes further, affirming his brotherhood with his offenders, declaring, "I am Joseph your brother, whom ye sold into Egypt."

Many, sadly, sever relationships and resist reconciliation due to their wounds. But love's test is the capacity to reach out to those who have wronged us before they even acknowledge their offenses. It is to radiate kindness and love even when the offender remains remorseful.

In verse 5, Joseph reassures his brothers, helping them

forgive themselves and see their actions in a different light, saying, "Now therefore be not grieved, nor angry with yourselves, that ye sold me hither: for God did send me before you to preserve life."

David: Kindness Personified

King David, too, displayed remarkable kindness. After enduring so much at the hands of King Saul, he demonstrated kindness to Saul's house. In 2 Samuel 9:1, David seeks to show kindness for Jonathan's sake, asking, "Is there yet any that is left of the house of Saul, that I may shew him kindness for Jonathan's sake?"

Instead of annihilating any potential threats to his throne, David honored the bond he shared with Jonathan by showing kindness to Saul's descendants. This action is a testament to the power of love and kindness that surpasses the instinct for self-preservation and revenge.

Our Savior, Jesus: Kindness Incarnate

Christ's life on Earth was a living testament to kindness. Matthew 8:1-3 records a powerful instance:

> "And behold, a leper came and worshiped Him, saying, 'Lord, if You are willing, You can make me clean.' Then Jesus put out His hand and touched him, saying, 'I am willing; be cleansed.' Immediately his leprosy was cleansed."

Kindness reaches out, putting the needs of others before self, and it is this that Jesus modeled.

From His interactions with sinners like Zacchaeus, the woman caught in adultery, or the Samaritan woman at the well, to His ultimate sacrifice on the cross, Jesus demonstrated the transformative power of kindness.

John 3:16 says, *"For God so loved the world, that he gave his only begotten Son, that whosoever believeth in him should not perish, but have everlasting life."*

This encapsulates God's kindness - a love so profound it reaches across the boundaries of sin and prejudice, offering salvation to all.

Let us be like Joseph, David, and Jesus, who embodied kindness. Even in the face of offense, let us not wait for the offender to express remorse but choose to love, forgive, and extend kindness. This is God's kind of love. This is genuine kindness.

Love Does Not Envy

The philosopher Harold Coffin once stated, "Envy is the art of counting the other fellow's blessings instead of your own."

Envy, as such, is the gnawing desire for what others have, a resentful craving ignited by their possessions or qualities. In essence, envy blinds us to our blessings as we belittle our worth and potential, amplifying the allure of others' achievements.

Envy was one of the insidious motives behind the crucifixion of our Lord Jesus Christ. Mark 15:9-14 depicts Pilate's knowing question, *"Do you want me to release to you the King of the Jews?"*

He understood that the chief priests were driven by envy to sacrifice Jesus, inciting the crowd to release Barabbas instead. Envy is a form of unloving covetousness, a destructive force that can lead to bitterness and hatred, particularly when we cannot emulate or possess the qualities we envy in others.

Envy Breeds Destruction

In the annals of the sacred text, envy has led to the taking of lives. Cain murdered Abel because God favored Abel's sacrifice. Envy fueled King Saul's relentless pursuit of David, driven by the people's praises for David's accomplishments. Esau, having received a lesser blessing than his brother Jacob, was driven by envy to plot his brother's demise.

Envy Diverts Focus

Envy distracts us from our achievements, leading us to fixate on the accomplishments of others. This is evident in 1 Samuel 18:7-9, where King Saul, incensed by the people's adulation of David, is consumed with envy, leading to murderous rage. His duties as king are neglected as he grows fixated on David, attempting to kill him in a fit of jealousy.

Your love will be tested when those around you seem more gifted. It will be challenging when others have what you lack. Other people's success and their stories of accomplishment may test your love. But remember, to pass the test of envy is to embrace love.

In Job 5:2, we are cautioned that *"wrath killeth the foolish man, and envy slayeth the silly one."*

Proverbs 23:17-18 implores us not to envy sinners but to fear the Lord, promising that our expectations shall not be cut off.

Psalm 37:1-3 encourages us not to fret over evildoers nor be envious of the workers of iniquity, reassuring us that if we trust in the Lord and do good, He will provide for us.

To Guard Against Envy

Consider these strategies for guarding against the spirit of envy:

- Reflect upon God's blessings in your life.
- Cultivate a spirit of gratitude for what you have.
- ·Resist the temptation to compare yourself to others.
- Embrace your uniqueness, understanding that we each have different capabilities and gifts.
- Find contentment in your unique qualities and life situation.
- Celebrate and rejoice in the success of others rather than begrudging them in their accomplishments.

This is love that does not envy - love that rejoices in the success of others, love that celebrates the uniqueness of each person, love that is content in its own skin, and love that does not diminish its own worth to magnify the allure of others' achievements. This is God's kind of love.

Love Does Not Put Others Down

The Apostle Paul writes in 1 Corinthians 13:4, *"charity vaunteth not itself, is not puffed up."* This admonition carries profound implications. The terms "vaunteth" and "puffed up" carry connotations of boasting and excessive self-praise.

These terms describe a haughty spirit that inflates itself above others through rhetorical exaggerations and vanity. Yet, this is not the character of love. Love does not seek to diminish others by magnifying itself.

In Philippians 2:3, we are instructed to conduct ourselves without strife or vainglory. Instead, we should adopt a humble mindset, esteeming others higher than ourselves.

Romans 12:10 echoes this sentiment, urging us to be affectionate towards one another with brotherly love, honoring and preferring one another in our interactions. The Apostle Peter adds to this in 1 Peter 5:5, advising us to submit to one another, putting on humility. He reminds us that God opposes the proud but gives grace to the humble.

Yet, there is a stark contrast between "feeling proud" and "being proud." Feeling proud is a positive emotion, an appreciative response to achievement, accomplishment, or commendable behavior in ourselves or others.

Being proud, however, can transform into a toxic arrogance that convinces us we are superior to others. This inflated self-perception often leads us to view others as less worthy, which directly contradicts the essence of love.

When we "vaunt" ourselves, framing our worth compared to others and treating them as inferior, we devalue them. But love is not a force of devaluation. Love does not degrade, cheapen, or undermine; it does not bring others down, diminish or debase them. Instead, love communicates worth, seeing and appreciating the inherent value in each individual.

Indeed, the Bible teaches us that love neither boasts nor belittles. Love neither inflates self-worth at the expense of others nor erodes the worth of others to enhance its own. Love, in its truest form, is humble, seeking not to put others down but to uplift, inspire, and see others not as competitors to surpass but as companions to cherish and esteem.

Love recognizes that each person is a unique creation, fearfully and wonderfully made in the image of God (Psalm 139:14). In the eyes of love, each individual possesses an irreplaceable value and a unique purpose. To love is to affirm this intrinsic worth, to celebrate it, and to treat each person with the dignity and respect they deserve as bearers of the divine image.

To practice such love is to align ourselves with the very heart of God, who is love (1 John 4:8). It is to cultivate a spirit of humility, esteem, and mutual respect, fostering a community where each person is honored, valued, and cherished. In doing so, we bear witness to the transformative power of love — a love that uplifts rather than puts down, fosters unity rather than division, and reflects the very character of God Himself.

Part 3 – Test of Character

Chapter 15

The True Test of Character

"Character cannot be developed in ease and quiet. Only through experience of trial and suffering can the soul be strengthened, vision cleared, ambition inspired, and success achieved." - Helen Keller

In an intriguing and perplexing spectacle of our modern era, we observe individuals who possess astounding gifts, with talent flowing as freely as rivers from their fingertips. They perform astonishing feats in the name of the Lord yet live lives strikingly at odds with the commandments and principles of God's word. Such individuals brandish their gifts like weapons, yet their personal lives bristle with conduct that offends the gospel.

In a confounding twist, many of these individuals seem blind to the contradictions within themselves. They gather legions of followers who admire their gifts and even deify them, glossing over the glaring discrepancies in their characters.

Beyond the Valley

The phrase, "touch not My anointed," is frequently wielded like a shield, quelling dissent, and intimidating any who dare to challenge or expose their inconsistencies.

These troubling observations are congruent with the warnings given by the Apostle Paul to his spiritual son, Timothy, concerning the spiritual climate of the last days. Paul's prophetic words resonate deeply with our contemporary reality:

> *"But know this, that in the last days perilous times will come: For men will be lovers of themselves, lovers of money, boasters, proud, blasphemers, disobedient to parents, unthankful, unholy, unloving, unforgiving, slanderers, without self-control, brutal, despisers of good, traitors, headstrong, haughty, lovers of pleasure rather than lovers of God, having a form of Godliness but denying its power. And from such people turn away!"* (2 Timothy 3:1-5)

> *"Now the Spirit expressly says that in latter times some will depart from the faith, giving heed to deceiving spirits and doctrines of demons, speaking lies in hypocrisy, having their own conscience seared with a hot iron, forbidding to marry, and commanding to abstain from foods which God created to be received with thanksgiving by those who believe and know the truth."* (1 Timothy 4:1-3)

This lifestyle is starkly antithetical to the character of Christ. It is not the path that Jesus walked during His earthly ministry. If He were among us today, He would not live in such a way.

Character is a moral compass, a beacon of integrity, a

fortress of ethical strength. It is the anchor that either secures us or renders us adrift in the turbulent sea of life. Whether we remain steadfast or waver under pressure largely depends on our character. I pray that you embody the character that reflects the model of Jesus.

Many Christians today seem more captivated by the gifts of the Spirit than the fruit of the Spirit. More discussion exists about the spectacular display of spiritual gifts than the cultivation of Godly character. Some believers are deemed "anointed" because of their gifts, as if character is not a manifestation of the anointing or as if there are separate anointings for gifts and character.

In His discourse about false prophets, Jesus declared, "You will know them by their fruits." (Matthew 7:16) He did not say that we would know them by their gifts. Jesus knew that even false prophets could manifest spiritual gifts. If we focus solely on these gifts, we risk being deceived. By their fruits—by their character traits—we shall recognize them.

> *"Beware of false prophets, who come to you in sheep's clothing, but inwardly they are ravenous wolves. You will know them by their fruits. Do men gather grapes from thornbushes or figs from thistles? Even so, every good tree bears good fruit, but a bad tree bears bad fruit. A good tree cannot bear bad fruit, nor can a bad tree bear good fruit. Every tree that does not bear good fruit is cut down and thrown into the fire. Therefore by their fruits you will know them."* (Matthew 7:15-20)

Jesus labeled them as false, as bad trees incapable of bearing good fruit. Nothing good can be expected from a bad source.

While even good people may occasionally stumble and make mistakes, a good tree—rooted in godly character—will consistently yield good fruits.

We need to be vigilant of the factors that corrupt godly character. The love of money is chief among them. Paul, in his letter to Timothy, warns of the dangers that lie in the pursuit of riches at the expense of character:

> "Now Godliness with contentment is great gain. For we brought nothing into this world, and it is certain we can carry nothing out. And having food and clothing, with these we shall be content. But those who desire to be rich fall into temptation and a snare, and into many foolish and harmful lusts which drown men in destruction and perdition. For the love of money is a root of all kinds of evil, for which some have strayed from the faith in their greediness, and pierced themselves through with many sorrows. But you, O man of God, flee these things and pursue righteousness, Godliness, faith, love, patience, gentleness." (1 Timothy 6:6-11)

Other corrupting influences include power, fame, success, and bad company. As the book of Proverbs insightfully states, "Whoever walks with the wise becomes wise, but the companion of fools will suffer harm." (Proverbs 13:20)

In these tumultuous times, when everything about us is tested, especially our character, we must remain rooted in our faith. These are times of uncertainty, despair, and yet also of hope. They are times of wisdom and foolishness, of abundance and want.

The accumulation of money, fame, and power places us in a

position where our character is tested. The real you is unveiled by how you treat people when you wield power. What do you do when no one is watching? Will you still adhere to the truth even if it brings trouble?

I have seen individuals who carried themselves with humility until success—particularly wealth—changed them drastically. They suddenly demanded reverence and submission, as if their newfound success made them superior to others.

In the following chapters, we will embark on a journey to examine some of God's champions from biblical history. We will delve into the tests they faced—tests that resonate with our present trials—and uncover the secrets of their victories. We will unearth the invaluable lessons that their lives offer for our character formation in these challenging times.

Chapter 16

Learning from Joseph

"Nothing of spiritual significance comes without sacrifice. Your spirituality will always be measured by the size of your sacrifice." - Jentezen Franklin

Joseph, son of Jacob, stands as a beacon, a figure cast in the luminous tapestry of biblical history. Following the lineage of Abraham, who proved his unwavering love for God through the willingness to sacrifice his cherished son, Isaac, we encounter Joseph.

Joseph is a paragon of character, a man whose story has echoed through generations, inspiring both the young and the old.

The tenth son of Jacob, Joseph was the firstborn of Rachel, the woman Jacob cherished above all others. He was the product of a long-awaited pregnancy, a symbol of patience rewarded, and love fulfilled.

The first glimpse of Joseph's destined greatness was evident when his father bestowed a coat of many colors upon him. This vibrant garment, saturated with hues as diverse as the challenges he would soon face, became a harbinger of his divine purpose.

Jacob's deep affection for Joseph, kindled by Rachel's struggle for motherhood and perhaps the unique qualities he saw in the boy, was unmistakable. It manifested in this remarkable coat, an emblem of favoritism that incited envy in his brothers. Joseph strutted with a spirit of greatness simply by donning this garment.

Despite the resentment simmering within his siblings, there was nothing that could alter God's plan. Such is the essence of divine work – when God marks an individual for greatness, no earthly power can interfere.

Coat of Many Colors

Garments in biblical times were more than mere clothing. They bore the weight of identity, symbolizing status, prowess, and virtue. They told stories of one's standing, hinted at accomplishments, and whispered of character.

A garment was not just worn but embodied, necessitating the wearer to live up to the honor it represented.

Let's look at several Biblical insights into what a garment represented to the Hebrews.

Garment of Honor and Beauty

Consider Aaron's sacred vestments, garments of honor and beauty. In the book of Exodus, we see the explicit instructions given by God to create these garments:

> *"And thou shalt make holy garments for Aaron thy brother for glory and for beauty. And thou shalt speak unto all that are wise hearted, whom I have filled with the spirit of wisdom, that they may make Aaron's garments to consecrate him, that he may minister unto me in the priest's office." (Exodus 28:2-3)*

These garments served a divine purpose. They were the robes of Aaron's priestly office, consecrating him for the sacred duty of serving God. The garments, imbued with glory and beauty, were not merely ornamental.

The term "glory" translates to "kâbôd" in Hebrew, suggesting heaviness or weightiness. It is a term that resonates with the concepts of wealth, abundance, importance, or respect. It evokes notions of honor, reputation, reverence, and dignity. The high priest, donned in these vestments, was required to embody the virtues his garments stood for. His character had to mirror the sanctity and nobility represented by his clothing.

Garment of Champions

Another role and meaning of garments is their link to being worn by a champion. This Garment of Champions is detailed in Judges 5:30:

> *"Have they not sped? have they not divided the prey; to every man a damsel or two; to Sisera a prey of divers colors, a prey of divers colors of needlework, of divers colors of needlework on both sides, meet for the necks of them that take the spoil?"*

Such attire was reserved for valiant men, those who exhibited strength, fortitude, and discipline in battle. Their triumphs were woven into their clothing, manifesting as colorful reminders of their victories.

Garment of Virtue

There is also a Garment of Virtue. In 2 Samuel 13:18-20, we learn of

> Tamar's plight.
> *Then he called his servant who attended him, and said, "Here! Put this woman out, away from me, and bolt the door behind her." Now she had on a robe of many colors, for the King's virgin daughters wore such apparel. And his servant put her out and bolted the door behind her. Then Tamar put ashes on her head, and tore her robe of many colors that was on her, and laid her hand on her head and went away crying bitterly. And Absalom her brother said to her, "Has Amnon your brother been with you? But now hold your peace, my sister. He is your brother; do not take this thing to heart." So Tamar remained desolate in her brother Absalom's house.* 2 Samuel 13:18-20

Her brother, Amnon, violated her, leaving her virtue compromised. Distraught, she tore her robe of many colors, symbolizing virginity, and purity. The rending of this garment signifies a loss of innocence, a tearing away of her purity. Once celebrated in her vibrant robe, her virtue was tragically stolen, leaving her desolate.

Garment of Access and Royalty

We also discover a Garment of Access and Royalty, described eloquently in Psalm 45:13-15:

> "The royal daughter is all glorious within the palace; Her clothing is woven with gold. She shall be brought to the King in robes of many colors; The virgins, her companions who follow her, shall be brought to You. With gladness and rejoicing they shall be brought; They shall enter the King's palace."

This apparel signifies outward glory and inner character, reminding us that true royalty lies within the soul. It is a garment that demands the wearer to be "glorious" within, echoing a consistent theme of character paralleling the grandeur of the garment.

Unfortunately, some covet the outward symbols of greatness without possessing the necessary inward qualities. Haman, for instance, in the Book of Esther, sought the adornment of the King's robes while harboring malicious intents. Such examples are a stark reminder that outward glory alone does not suffice; it must be accompanied by inward integrity and character.

Joseph's life exemplifies this theme. He was frequently associated with garments, either receiving them as tokens of love and status or being stripped of them in deceit and malice. Yet, his outer garments did not define his greatness. His integrity remained intact, even when his physical attire was forcibly removed.

In Genesis 41:42-43, after his faithful stewardship and

refusal to be embittered by his tribulations, Joseph is once again robed, this time by Pharaoh:

> *"Then Pharaoh took his signet ring off his hand and put it on Joseph's hand; and he clothed him in garments of fine linen and put a gold chain around his neck. And he had him ride in the second chariot which he had; and they cried out before him, "Bow the knee!" So he set him over all the land of Egypt."*

Joseph's life and trials are a testament to the value of unwavering character, even in the face of extreme adversity. Despite being stripped of his garments multiple times, the continuity of his integrity offers a profound lesson. His story is a poignant reminder that though external recognitions are noteworthy, it is one's internal character that truly defines their worth.

Sadly, today's ministry often encounters individuals seeking outward recognition and honor without having to prove their character. They long for titles and acknowledgments while contributing little to the Kingdom of God.

They show more love for themselves than God, lacking the godly character to warrant the honor they covet. Joseph's journey reminds us of the importance of a tested, proven character, for it is character, above all else, that makes one worthy of honor and status.

The biblical emphasis on garments is much more than a superficial focus on clothing. It is an allegory, underscoring the deep connection between outward symbols and inward virtues, between physical attire and moral character. In Biblical narrative, garments are not merely worn; they are inhabited.

To don a garment, be it one of champions, virtue, or royalty, one must embody the qualities it represents, a challenge that invites each of us to strive for moral excellence and spiritual growth.

Early Evidence of Greatness

Joseph's life was always connected to dreams. Visions, like delicate threads in the weave of his existence, set him apart and marked him for God's purpose, but they also became a beacon for the storms in his life.

In his first dream, as they stood in the fields, his brothers' sheaves bowed low before his. The second, more incendiary dream is chronicled in Genesis 37:9-11:

> *"Then he dreamed still another dream and told it to his brothers, and said, "Look, I have dreamed another dream. And this time, the sun, the moon, and the eleven stars bowed down to me." So he told it to his father and his brothers; and his father rebuked him and said to him, "What is this dream that you have dreamed? Shall your mother and I and your brothers indeed come to bow down to the earth before you?" And his brothers envied him, but his father kept the matter in mind."*

As these dreams unfurled like banners over his destiny, Joseph's brethren were consumed by envy. Yet, Jacob, his father, marked these celestial visions. He perceived the hand of divine selection on his son and held these prophetic signs like cherished secrets in his heart.

But not everyone treasured these glimpses of Joseph's future greatness. His brothers, fueled by envy and hatred, conspired against him. Their love for him had evaporated into cold malice. Such is the cautionary tale when we reveal our dreams to others.

Among us are dream-killers, those whose own bitterness and resentment would seek to snuff out the spark of potential in others. Wisdom, often the fruit of painful experience, counsels us to guard our dreams, sharing them only with those who would nurture rather than extinguish them.

The plot against Joseph thickened when they saw him approach from afar. Genesis 37:18-20 illustrates the malevolence that had consumed his brothers:

> *"Now when they saw him afar off, even before he came near them, they conspired against him to kill him. Then they said to one another, "Look, this dreamer is coming! Come therefore, let us now kill him and cast him into some pit; and we shall say, 'Some wild beast has devoured him.' We shall see what will become of his dreams!"*

This heinous plot, born of envy and resentment, resulted in Joseph being cast into a pit and later sold into slavery. Reuben could not bear the thought of bloodshed; hence, the decision to cast him into the pit instead of killing him outright. Later, they pulled him from his dark prison only to condemn him to another - a life of servitude in the land of Egypt, sold to passing traders like a common chattel.

Joseph's tale is an arresting study of the trials one might face when marked for greatness. It reminds us that the path to fulfilling our God-given destiny can be fraught with challenges, and yet, as Joseph's story will later reveal, the dreams planted in our hearts are far from fragile; they are resilient seeds, capable of blooming even in the harshest of circumstances.

Honored in Potiphar's House

Having been sold into the very heart of Egypt, Joseph found himself in the house of Potiphar, an officer of Pharaoh, the captain of the guard. Yet, despite the chains of his predicament, Joseph carried within him something more potent than iron fetters - he bore the anointing of God upon his life.

This is vividly illuminated in Genesis 39:1-6:

> *"Now Joseph had been taken down to Egypt. And Potiphar, an officer of Pharaoh, captain of the guard, an Egyptian, bought him from the Ishmaelites who had taken him down there. The LORD was with Joseph, and he was a successful man; and he was in the house of his master the Egyptian. And his master saw that the LORD was with him and that the LORD made all he did to prosper in his hand. So Joseph found favor in his sight, and served him. Then he made him overseer of his house, and all that he had he put under his authority. So it was, from the time that he had made him overseer of his house and all that he had, that the LORD blessed the Egyptian's house for Joseph's sake; and the blessing of the LORD was on all that he had in the house and in the field. Thus he left all that he had in Joseph's hand, and he did not know what he had except for the bread which he ate."*

The spirit of this passage is suffused with divine favor. Joseph, while bearing the title of a slave, was no ordinary man in bondage. His presence was transformative. If one were to demean a man upon whom the Spirit of God rested, especially when this man caused all things in your house to flourish, you might question your judgment. This was the puzzle that confronted Potiphar: how should he regard this extraordinary individual?

In recognition of his extraordinary abilities, Potiphar elevated Joseph above all others in his house, bar his wife. The slave was thus transformed into an authoritative figure, shifting the balance of his existence. But with this newfound status came the temptation and trials that often accompany power and prestige.

Test of Purity

The test of character, a crucible for purity, is a trial that has seen many of God's servants stumble, and Joseph was no exception. Even the righteous are not immune to the allure of temptation. Genesis 39:7-10 details the seductive attempts of Potiphar's wife:

> "Now Joseph was handsome in form and appearance. And it came to pass after these things that his master's wife cast longing eyes on Joseph, and she said, "Lie with me." But he refused and said to his master's wife, "Look, my master does not know what is with me in the house, and he has committed all that he has to my hand. There is no one greater in this house than I, nor has he kept back anything from me but you, because you are his wife. How then can I do this great wickedness, and sin against God?" So it was, as she spoke to Joseph day by day, that he did not heed her, to lie with her or to be with her."

Joseph was caught in a tormenting tempest, a handsome young man adorned with power, ceaselessly solicited by his master's wife. The siren's song echoed through the house, a continual whisper in his ear, "Come, lie with me."

It might have been tempting to shrug and think, 'God would understand; the burden is too heavy.' But Joseph's honor and faith were steadfast, carved from the same stone as his commitment to God. He echoed his refusal, underlining the violation it would be against both his master and his God.

Joseph's reference to Potiphar's wife as "his wife" revealed a profound respect for the sanctity of marriage. This was not just a wrong against man, but a "great wickedness, and sin against God."

His primary motivation was to honor God, even above Potiphar. His actions weren't driven by a fear of earthly punishment or the distant hope of his brothers' obeisance but rather by an unwavering commitment to God and His principles. This resolve, an unyielding fidelity to righteousness, was Joseph's fortress in the face of temptation.

Ultimately, Joseph endured the harsh consequences of a false accusation rather than succumbing to illicit pleasure. He understood the dangers of becoming enslaved not just to a man but to the seductive grip of sin.

Test of Forgiveness

By standing steadfast in his commitment to God, Joseph found himself in prison. His path to greatness was littered with challenges, yet his integrity and faith in God remained resolute. His commitment to God's principles was the lighthouse guiding him through the stormy seas of his trials.

Within the bleak walls of the prison, Joseph found an unexpected stage for his God-given gift. Dreams, those ethereal fragments of subconscious thought, began to pervade the minds of his fellow prisoners.

The King's butler, and his cupbearer, incarcerated alongside Joseph, were the first to experience these perplexing visions. God spoke through Joseph, gifting him with accurate interpretations. As the narratives of their dreams unfolded, one prisoner was released and restored while the other met a grim fate, just as Joseph had predicted.

Yet, the divine theatre of dreams didn't end there. The King himself was visited by two enigmatic dreams, echoes of the same theme. In response, Joseph was summoned from his cell, the chains of his bondage momentarily forgotten. He interpreted the King's dreams and even provided a solution to the problem they outlined. His reward? A sudden, meteoric rise from a slave of Potiphar to the Prime Minister of Egypt, a trajectory almost inconceivable.

As Joseph's status climbed, his past as a slave faded into obscurity. He was no longer a captive but Egypt's second most powerful man.

The winds of fate shifted once again with the onset of famine, leading Joseph's brothers to seek grain in Egypt. After a series of encounters and eventual revelations, the family was reunited in Egypt, settling in the fertile region of Goshen. Over time, their father, Jacob, passed away.

One would expect bitterness, a thirst for revenge, to bubble within Joseph, particularly toward Potiphar and his wife. Yet, the records show no trace of it. No vendetta, no payback, only silence. If this resilience surprises you, a more profound test awaited Joseph.

A lingering fear crept among Joseph's brothers as Jacob's life concluded. Would the wrongs they committed come back to haunt them? The narrative in Genesis 50:15-21 unravels this tension:

> *"When Joseph's brothers saw that their father was dead, they said, 'Perhaps Joseph will hate us, and may actually repay us for all the evil which we did to him.' So they sent messengers to Joseph, saying, 'Before your father died he commanded, saying, 'Thus you shall say to Joseph: 'I beg you, please forgive the trespass of your brothers and their sin; for they did evil to you.' ' Now, please, forgive the trespass of the servants of the God of your father.' And Joseph wept when they spoke to him."*

Fear and guilt drove Joseph's brothers to their knees before him. Yet, his response? "Do not be afraid, for am I in the place of God? But as for you, you meant evil against me; but God meant it for good, in order to bring it about as it is this day, to save many people alive. Now, therefore, do not be afraid; I will provide for you and your little ones."

Joseph not only forgave but comforted them, proving that he had passed the second character test – forgiveness.

Joseph's life poses a question to all of us. When faced with a person from our past who wronged us, do we hold onto resentment, or do we choose the path of forgiveness? Do we let past wrongs dictate our actions, or do we, like Joseph, recognize God's greater design at play? Joseph's story serves as a humbling reminder of the strength of character required to truly forgive. Are we willing to learn from it?

Reuben Denied Patriarchal Blessing

Towards the end of his life, the patriarch Jacob bestowed upon his children prophetic blessings that would reverberate through their future generations. Each son received words of affirmation, admonition, and hope.

However, for Reuben, the firstborn, it was a tragic denunciation. His failure to uphold virtue led to him missing the patriarchal blessing, an affirmation typically bestowed by fathers upon their children before death.

The book of Genesis chapter 49, verses 3 and 4, records Jacob's stern words:

> *"Reuben, you are my firstborn, my might and the beginning of my strength, the excellency of dignity and the excellency of power. Unstable as water, you shall not excel, because you went up to your father's bed; then you defiled it—He went up to my couch."*

Once the heir apparent of Jacob's legacy, Reuben stood in disgrace because he did not pass the test that Joseph overcame with integrity in Potiphar's house. Reuben's impulsive act of sleeping with his father's concubine cost him his position and prestige. It was a sharp, cutting reminder of the consequences of failing to uphold one's moral responsibility.

In contrast, Joseph's testament stood stark and splendid. Having passed the test of character, he had his honor restored.

Through Pharaoh's favor, the vestments of status and dignity were returned to him. His trajectory, from the depths of a pit to the heights of Egypt's power structure, was a tangible sign of his steadfast character and unyielding faith.

The sin of fornication and adultery, a stumbling block that caused Reuben's downfall, was the same sin Joseph astutely avoided. Such sins are not to be taken lightly. Like Joseph, our generation must perceive them as wickedness and use all the strength and wisdom God grants us to steer clear of them.

Just as the contrasting destinies of Reuben and Joseph were dictated by their responses to moral tests, so are our lives shaped by our choices. The question we must pose to ourselves is simple yet profound: In moments of moral dilemma, will we succumb like Reuben or stand firm like Joseph? The answer to this question carries far-reaching implications, determining whether we receive our due blessings or forfeit them to our failures.

Chapter 17

The Rigors of Righteousness

"What lies behind us and what lies before us are tiny matters compared to what lies within us." - Ralph Waldo Emerson

The scriptures present the character of Job in shining light, depicting him as a man of great wealth, influence, and righteousness. Within the sacred pages of the Bible, Job's story unfurls amidst the sands of Uz, a land far removed from the Jewish milieu of Israel. Despite his geographic and cultural distance from the chosen people, Job's fear of God and moral uprightness garnered divine attention and favor.

The first chapter of Job paints a vivid picture of his prosperity,

"There was a man in the land of Uz, whose name was Job; and that man was blameless and upright, and one who feared God and shunned evil. His possessions were seven thousand sheep,

three thousand camels, five hundred yoke of oxen, five hundred female donkeys, and a very large household, so that this man was the greatest of all the people of the East." (Job 1:1-3)

Truly, Job's life reflected a tableau of abundance and virtuous living. However, as Job would learn, such abundance would be a double-edged sword. The divine favor that brought him much comfort would soon plunge him into an ocean of trials.

It all began when God proudly acknowledged Job's righteousness before Satan, the ultimate accuser. *"Have you considered My servant Job, that there is none like him on the earth, a blameless and upright man, one who fears God and shuns evil?"* (Job 1:8).

God's effusive praise of Job's uprightness enticed the adversary to challenge the authenticity of Job's devotion.

Although Job was not of Israelite lineage and likely lacked the theological knowledge of the God of Abraham, Isaac, and Jacob, he carried an innate reverence for God. His god-fearing character was not derived from religious instruction but from a moral compass guided by the divine light within his spirit. A light that shone brightly enough to catch God's approving gaze.

God's commendations of Job were not random expressions of divine satisfaction. They were divine endorsements of Job's righteousness, repeated testimonials of a man deemed perfect and upright by God Himself. Such divine authentication is rarely found in biblical history, marking Job as a figure of unique spiritual significance.

The narrative of Job conveys to us the essential truth that God's approval is not predicated on material prosperity or worldly fame. Indeed, these worldly accolades often lead to the downfall of those who once stood tall. God measures us not by our possessions or talents but by the strength and purity of our character.

Your reputation might lie in the hands of others, subject to their whims and opinions, but your character, the essence of who you are, remains within your control. This internal substance, this moral architecture, sets you apart in God's eyes. It is not your spirituality, prayers, or scripture knowledge that distinguishes you but your character.

In the divine scheme of things, what people think of you matters little; what truly counts is who you are at your core. God, the discerner of the heart's deepest thoughts and intents, looks beyond the outward show to the inner being. And it is here, in the recesses of your heart and the integrity of your character, that God's gaze lingers, seeking the reflection of His divine image.

Satan Takes Advantage

The adversary, ever cunning and treacherous, sought to exploit Job's blessings as his Achilles heel. He dared to suggest that Job's integrity was tethered to his wealth, asserting that should this bounty be taken away, Job's fidelity to God would crumble.

A man's worth in Job's society hinged not only on his wealth but also on the number of his offspring; hence, Satan sought to dismantle both pillars of Job's standing.

Indeed, the enemy often attacks those things we hold dear, those aspects of our lives that shape our sense of worth. We must steadfastly uphold our testimony before the Lord, refusing to let the enemy's machinations alter our character or faith.

The enemy is not always a visible foe; he sometimes operates through those closest to us. In Job's case, his wife, and friends, misguided by their understanding of his tribulations, became unwitting agents of Satan. Job had to decide whose interpretation he would heed - the perspectives of his loved ones or the hidden workings of God.

Job's Character Stands Firm

What set Job apart during this harrowing ordeal was his unwavering character. His response to adversity was not laced with blame or anger but acceptance and reverence. *"Naked I came from my mother's womb, and naked shall I return there. The LORD gave, and the LORD has taken away; Blessed be the name of the LORD."* (Job 1:21). In all this, Job did not sin nor charge God with wrong (Job 1:22).

The true test of character is not just what we do but what we say, especially in the face of adversity. Too often, our words have sown discord and pain, leaving lasting scars on those we care about. In this realm, Job proved exceptional, exercising restraint and wisdom in his speech even in the darkest moments.

His unwavering control of speech garnered the praise of the Apostle James, who wrote, *"For we all stumble in many things. If anyone does not stumble in word, he is a perfect man, able also to bridle the whole body."* (James 3:2). Job mastered the art of taming his tongue, never allowing his words to dishonor God.

Furthermore, Job demonstrated admirable respect and kindness to those under his care, acknowledging their shared humanity and divine creation. He treated his servants justly, cared for the poor, and attended to the needs of the widow and the fatherless. Such was the strength of his character that even when his life was in turmoil, his concern for others never wavered.

How do we treat those under our care? Would our house helps, drivers, or subordinates vouch for our kindness? These are pivotal questions we must ask ourselves, for our treatment of those who serve us is a vital test of our character.

Finally, Job's story is a testament to the divine rewards for an unshakeable character. God blessed Job's latter days more than his beginning (Job 42:12). His wealth was restored, his family multiplied, and he lived a long life, full of days. This shows us that we earn divine approval and blessings when we stand firm in our character and hold steadfast in our faith despite life's trials. Praise be to God.

Progressive Affirmation of Job's Character

As we have seen, God, in His omnipotent wisdom, drew the adversary's attention to His servant Job, who exemplified righteousness in the land of Uz.

The divine narrative offers an intimate portrayal of Job's character:

> "There was a man in the land of Uz, whose name was Job; and that man was perfect and upright, and one that feared God, and eschewed evil." Job 1:1

Notice how God highlighted four sterling qualities in Job:

Perfection - This does not imply sinlessness but rather denotes a state of maturity and completeness.

Uprightness - A trait reflecting an individual who is straight, balanced, and pleasing in his actions.

Fear of God - Job was not terrified of God. Instead, he reverenced and respected Him, humbly acknowledging God's power and authority.

Eschewing evil - Job was steadfast in shunning sin, consistently turning aside from evil.

As the narrative progresses, God's estimation of Job ascends to a higher level, elevating his moral and spiritual character even further.

"Hast thou considered my servant Job, that there is none like him in the earth, a perfect and an upright man, one that feareth God, and escheweth evil?" (Job 1:8)

An additional trait is unveiled in Job - distinction. There was none like him on Earth.

In the aftermath of Satan's assault on Job's wealth and family, Job's response was a beacon of his resolute faith and unflinching character.

"Then Job arose, and rent his mantle, and shaved his head, and fell down upon the ground, and worshipped... Naked came I out of my mother's womb, and naked shall I return thither: the LORD gave, and the LORD hath taken away; blessed be the name of the LORD. In all this Job sinned not, nor charged God foolishly." Job 1:20-22

Amid the storm of loss and sorrow, Job's reverence for God remained steadfast. His suffering did not alter his perception of God, and he neither sinned nor blamed his Maker.

Once again, the divine testimony of Job evolves:

"And the LORD said unto Satan, Hast thou considered my servant Job, that there is none like him in the earth, a perfect and an upright man, one that fears God, and eschews evil? and still he holds fast his integrity, although you move me against him, to destroy him without cause." Job 2:3

Job's character now held a sixth dimension - he held fast to his integrity, regardless of the trials he endured.

Can we, like Job, maintain our integrity when the world crumbles around us? Can our characters withstand the fiery trials of loss and pain? Will we remain faithful when our blessings seem to dwindle, and our joy is shrouded by sorrow?

Job's story teaches us that the true measure of our character is revealed not in times of prosperity but in the crucible of affliction. He faced the loss of family and wealth, endured his wife's misguided advice to curse God, and navigated through the muddled counsel of his friends.

Once revered by the young and old alike, Job was now overlooked. He mourned the days when princes held their tongues and the nobles silenced themselves in his presence. Yet, despite the profound losses and the painful trials, Job held fast to his character and faith.

With every trial, Job's virtues shone brighter, revealing his indomitable spirit. The more the refiner's fire burned, the more the gold within him was purified. His story beckons us to reflect on our own journey and challenges us to hold fast to our integrity, no matter how fierce the storms of life may rage.

The Final Call - Integrity Amidst Trials

In the concluding verses of Job's story, we glean precious wisdom that anchors our faith, even as the waves of adversity seek to upend us. Just like Job's, the storms that we encounter in life are often ferocious, threatening to sweep us away. Yet it is precisely during these tempestuous times that our true character is laid bare, revealing either a steadfast resolve or a faltering spirit.

The essence of Job's story rests not in his suffering but in his persistent faith, steadfast integrity, and unyielding reverence for God. His trials did not lead him to blame God; instead, they solidified his faith. Herein lies a critical lesson: our attitude toward God must never be conditional on our circumstances.

In times of prosperity, it is easy to shower God with praises. Yet when adversity strikes, wealth dwindles, health fails, and loved ones depart, will we, like Job, still fall to our knees and say, "Blessed be the name of the Lord"?

Our calling, then, is to emulate Job's unwavering integrity. Let us strive to live upright lives, irrespective of our circumstances. As we face life's trials, may we remember that the God we serve is more interested in refining our character than shielding us from all discomfort. Let us turn our trials into opportunities for growth, allowing them to shape us into more mature, compassionate, and righteous individuals.

Moreover, let us remember our responsibilities towards our fellow human beings. Job treated everyone with dignity and respect, regardless of their social standing. This should urge us to examine our own interactions. How do we treat those who work for us or with us? Are we showing kindness to our drivers, house helpers, or the young intern at our workplace?

Job's story is a clarion call for us to remember that every individual we encounter is created in the image of God. To mistreat them is to disrespect the Creator. So, let us ensure our words and actions reflect our recognition of their inherent worth, whether we are a CEO or a cleaning staff.

Lastly, let us always remember Job's outcome - restoration beyond what was lost. The trials we endure are but for a moment. Like Job, we, too, can look forward to a time of restoration and reward. Let our present struggles serve as a testament to our unwavering faith, building in us a steadfast spirit and a character pleasing to God.

Let's take a moment to ponder on the lessons from Job's life. In the face of adversity, let us remember who we are and, more importantly, Whose we are. Let us draw strength from our faith, uphold our integrity, and never cease to extend love and kindness to all. Above all, let us never lose sight of the ultimate reward - the joy of pleasing God through our enduring faith and character.

Chapter 18

The Making of a Queen

"*Adversity does not build character, it reveals it.*" - James Lane Allen

Among the stories of faith, the story of Esther, a Jewish woman of extraordinary character, rises like a beacon, guiding us in the path of integrity. Esther, who rose from humble beginnings as a captive in Persia, was handpicked by God to serve a greater purpose. The road that led her to the throne of Persia was paved with trials, faith, and an unyielding commitment to her people and her God.

The royal backdrop to Esther's story is introduced with Queen Vashti's disobedience. In Esther 1:9-12, we find Vashti feasting in the king's palace, which she occupied solely because of her union with the king.

Queen Vashti also made a feast for the women in the royal palace which belonged to King Ahasuerus. On the seventh day,

when the heart of the king was merry with wine, he commanded Mehuman, Biztha, Harbona, Bigtha, Abagtha, Zethar, and Carcas, seven eunuchs who served in the presence of King Ahasuerus, to bring Queen Vashti before the king, wearing her royal crown, in order to show her beauty to the people and the officials, for she was beautiful to behold. But Queen Vashti refused to come at the king's command brought by his eunuchs; therefore the king was furious, and his anger burned within him.
Esther 1:9-12

When summoned by her king, Queen Vashi refused to come, a public defiance that burned like a slap in the king's face. It was not merely the king she disrespected but the very institution of kingship, the symbol of power and order in the Persian kingdom.

Such audacity, while shocking, holds within it a lesson for us. Position, wealth, and influence are never a license to dishonor or disregard those through whom these blessings flow. Remember, Vashti was a queen, not by her merit, but by her marriage to the king.

In our lives, our blessings and positions are often not of our making but gifts from God, our King. Let us be careful not to act like Vashti, treating our blessings with arrogance, lest we face the consequences.

The royal council persuaded the king to dismiss her, foreseeing the chaos that Vashti's behavior could incite in their homes. Thus, the throne of Persia was left without a queen, creating a vacuum only destiny could fill.

Esther Promoted to Power as Queen

Enter Esther, a young Jewish maiden known then as Hadassah. Brought up by her wise and godly uncle, Mordecai, she was ushered into the fray, a selection process that would see a new queen ascend the throne. Esther 2:15-18 depicts Esther's entrance into the royal palace.

> *Now when the turn came for Esther the daughter of Abihail the uncle of Mordecai, who had taken her as his daughter, to go in to the king, she requested nothing but what Hegai the king's eunuch, the custodian of the women, advised. And Esther obtained favor in the sight of all who saw her. So Esther was taken to King Ahasuerus, into his royal palace, in the tenth month, which is the month of Tebeth, in the seventh year of his reign. 17 The king loved Esther more than all the other women, and she obtained grace and favor in his sight more than all the virgins; so he set the royal crown upon her head and made her queen instead of Vashti. Then the king made a great feast, the Feast of Esther, for all his officials and servants; and he proclaimed a holiday in the provinces and gave gifts according to the generosity of a king.* Esther 2:15-18

Esther came with no fanfare, no demands. She asked only for what Hegai, the custodian of women, suggested. It was in her simplicity, humility, and obedience that Esther found favor in the eyes of all who saw her.

Love blossomed in the king's heart for Esther, not merely for her external beauty but for her inner grace. Thus, Esther was crowned queen, succeeding Vashti. A new chapter in the

Persian court was inaugurated with the Feast of Esther, a testament to her favor and the king's joy.

Reflect on the path that led Esther from obscurity to the royal court. Was it not the hand of God, guiding her, elevating her, preparing her for a divine purpose? Esther's ascent to the throne echoes the journey of Joseph, another captive who rose to prominence in a foreign land.

Such stories remind us that no matter our current circumstances, God can and will use us for His purposes. If we maintain our character and faith, like Esther, we will find favor in the eyes of God and man.

Thus, the story of Esther serves as a potent reminder: Favor follows the faithful, and destiny awaits those who honor God and their fellow humans with integrity and humility. As we continue exploring the virtues that defined Esther's character, let us be inspired to emulate her faith, courage, and humility.

The Silent Power of Humility: Testing the Character

Continuing our journey through the chronicles of Esther, we find her in the crosshairs of a vile conspiracy. Esther, once a mere captive, now the queen of Persia, had unknowingly become the target of Haman's malevolence.

Aggrieved by Mordecai's refusal to bow before him, Haman had contrived a deadly scheme to annihilate all Jews in the kingdom and to hang Mordecai. This was the crucible in which Esther's character was tested, a test that hinged on her humility and courage.

Beyond the Valley

The conversation recorded in Esther 4:13-16 captures the gravity of the situation and the stakes involved.

And Mordecai told them to answer Esther: "Do not think in your heart that you will escape in the king's palace any more than all the other Jews. For if you remain completely silent at this time, relief and deliverance will arise for the Jews from another place, but you and your father's house will perish. Yet who knows whether you have come to the kingdom for such a time as this?" Then Esther told them to reply to Mordecai: "Go, gather all the Jews who are present in Shushan, and fast for me; neither eat nor drink for three days, night or day. My maids and I will fast likewise, and so I will go to the king, which is against the law; and if I perish, I perish!

Mordecai, a man of discernment, cautioned Esther against the delusion of safety within the palace walls. He pointed to the divine providence that may have positioned her as queen for such a time as this to bring deliverance to her people.

Esther's response reverberates with the echo of her profound humility and faith. Not only did she grasp the gravity of Mordecai's message, but she also leaned into her roots as a Jew, rallying her people to fast and pray with her for three days. It was an act of humility, demonstrating her awareness of her dependence on God's favor, even as queen.

Now it happened on the third day that Esther put on her royal robes and stood in the inner court of the king's palace, across from the king's house, while the king sat on his royal throne in the royal house, facing the entrance of the house. So it was, when the king saw Queen Esther standing in the court, that she found favor in his sight, and the king held out to Esther the golden scepter that was in his hand. Then Esther went near and touched the top of the scepter. Esther 5:1-2

In Esther 5:1-2, we witness Esther, adorned in her royal robes, standing in the inner court of the king's palace. It was a perilous moment, laden with uncertainty, yet, when the king saw Esther, she found favor in his sight. He extended the golden scepter towards her, a gesture of acceptance and respect, inviting her to approach.

Esther's demeanor, in contrast to Vashti's, is instructive. Whereas Vashti had disrespected the king and his command, Esther had sought the king's and the Lord's favor. She respected the royal protocol and waited patiently for the king's approval to approach him. This humble, respectful approach starkly contrasted with Vashti's defiant attitude, showcasing the depth of Esther's character.

In the face of power and influence, Esther did not lose her humility or cease seeking counsel. Mordecai, her wise and godly uncle, remained her mentor, her voice of reason. Unlike Vashti, who had no Mordecai, Esther was humble enough to receive advice and guidance, demonstrating the true character of a queen.

Indeed, as we ascend the ladder of success and influence, we should never allow our position to inflate our pride or diminish our humility. We should always have someone like Mordecai in our lives, someone wise and godly who can guide us, counsel us, and speak the truth into our lives.

As the narrative unfolds, Esther, displaying wisdom and

humility, makes her request to the king. She did not rant against Haman. Instead, she invited the king to a feast she had prepared, demonstrating graciousness and respect in stark contrast to Vashti's rebellious attitude.

Esther's conduct is a lesson in wielding power with wisdom and humility. Even though the king offered her half his kingdom, she remained humble and respectful, understanding that her position was a gift from God.

In the end, Esther did not perish. The Jews were saved, Mordecai was spared, and Haman was hanged, a divine twist in the narrative. This was the triumph of a woman who had stood the test and shown that power coupled with humility and wisdom can transform destinies and save nations.

Esther's Triumph

And so, the tale of Esther, the Jewish maiden turned queen of Persia, concludes not in tragedy but in triumph, a testament to her humility, courage, and wisdom. Yet it is more than a mere chronicle of Esther's journey; it is a guidebook for those who aspire to handle power and influence with grace and godliness.

The narrative of Esther teaches us that our strength does not lie solely in our power or influence but in our humility, our willingness to seek advice, and our unwavering trust in God. Esther did not let her position as queen distract her from her roots or faith. She held firm to her beliefs, even in the face of potential death. As such, she provides a profound example of how to navigate positions of power with integrity and humility.

Esther's story serves as a call to those in power to never forsake their values, to never forget the importance of humility, and to never underestimate the significance of wise counsel. Those elevated to positions of influence should ensure they have a 'Mordecai' in their lives - a wise mentor who can guide them, provide perspective, and ensure they remain grounded in their values.

The tale also admonishes us about the consequences of pride and the reckless misuse of power, as embodied by Vashti. Her dismissal and downfall are stark warnings that power without humility can lead to one's ruin.

The story of Esther is a timeless narrative of character, courage, and conviction. It serves as an enduring reminder that those who remain true to their values and humble in their conduct, even in the face of immense power and influence, can truly make a difference.

It is a testament to the fact that when we place our trust in God and align ourselves with His will, even the seemingly insurmountable trials can be overcome, transforming threats into triumphs and despair into deliverance.

Chapter 19

The Mettle of Daniel

"Character is like a tree and reputation like its shadow. The shadow is what we think of it; the tree is the real thing." - Abraham Lincoln

In the iridescent mosaic of biblical narratives, the story of Daniel stands as a parable of unwavering faith, tested character, and resilient spirit. As we dive into his story etched in the sands of Babylon and crystallized in the annals of God's Word, we encounter a young man, far from his homeland, navigating the treacherous currents of captivity, yet destined for greatness.

This is the tale of Daniel - an emblem of virtue and a testament to the power of enduring character in the face of adversity. Steeped in the echoes of foreign tongues and enmeshed in a tapestry of strange customs, Daniel was a Hebrew youth ripped from the comforting familiarity of his homeland and thrust into the gleaming court of Babylonian royalty.

His lineage held no royal privilege; his youth was not cradled in the silk of nobility. Yet, it was this very young man who, without the armor of privilege, rose to unprecedented heights in a realm that was not his own. And in doing so, he laid bare a strength of character that transcended earthly dominions and bore the stamp of God's favor.

From the shimmering palaces of Babylon to the unfathomable depths of the lions' den, Daniel's journey was riddled with both trials and triumphs. His story is not merely a chronicle of his rise to prominence amidst chaos and uncertainty; it is an enduring testament to the invincible power of character molded by steadfast character and humble devotion.

As we delve into this chapter, we invite you to step into Daniel's shoes, feel the sands of Babylon beneath your feet, and witness the unfolding of an extraordinary narrative that transcends time and space.

The opening verses of the first chapter of Daniel present us with a curious scenario. The Babylonian king, Nebuchadnezzar, issued an order that fundamentally altered the trajectory of Daniel's life.

> *"Then the king instructed Ashpenaz, the master of his eunuchs, to bring some of the children of Israel and some of the king's descendants and some of the nobles, young men in whom there was no blemish, but good-looking, gifted in all wisdom, possessing knowledge and quick to understand, who had ability to serve in the king's palace, and whom they might teach the language and literature of the Chaldeans." Daniel 1:3-4*

It was a somber decree, yet it served as the conduit that

unveiled Daniel's greatness. Daniel and a handful of other Hebrew boys were singled out among the captives - plucked from obscurity and thrust into the epicenter of Babylonian civilization.

To the discerning eye, these young men exhibited signs of uncommon promise. They were free of physical blemish, handsome in appearance, blessed with wisdom beyond their years, quick to comprehend, and capable of serving in the king's court.

Furthermore, they were to be immersed in the language and literature of the Chaldeans. This was a test of their adaptability, a crucible designed to refine their natural abilities and transform them into instruments of the Babylonian court.

From these humble beginnings, the story of Daniel, the captive turned advisor, begins to unfold. His trials in Babylon, from the lion's den to the king's court, become the tapestry upon which his remarkable character is intricately woven.

Proving Mettle through Loyalty to Godly Tenets

The landscape of life is littered with challenges, both trivial and monumental. Daniel and his companions' first trial on the path to eminence tested their commitment to the godly values ingrained in their hearts during their formative years in Israel.

The royal Babylonian table was abundant with a plethora of exotic dishes, yet the Hebrew boys stood steadfast in their resolve not to defile themselves with the king's food.

Their choice seemed absurd, even dangerous, in the foreign court. Yet, when the test was concluded, they emerged healthier, their vitality untouched, their commitment unbroken. It prompts us to question: In a world rich with temptations and diversions, do we possess the strength to adhere to our convictions, regardless of our surroundings?

Daniel and his friends were not intimidated or swayed; they embodied their faith despite adversity. Their commitment to their principles didn't go unnoticed, nor was it unrewarded. Daniel's excellence, unparalleled wisdom, and insight propelled him into the spotlight. His name echoed through the palace hallways, resonating with a reputation of integrity and intellect.

> *"Then this Daniel distinguished himself above the governors and satraps, because an excellent spirit was in him; and the king gave thought to setting him over the whole realm. So the governors and satraps sought to find some charge against Daniel concerning the kingdom; but they could find no charge or fault, because he was faithful; nor was there any error or fault found in him. Then these men said, "We shall not find any charge against this Daniel unless we find it against him concerning the law of his God.""* Daniel 6:3-5

Yet, success is often accompanied by envy. Daniel's rise in influence and exceptional spirit ignited a flame of jealousy among the Babylonian officials. They conspired against him, scrutinizing his actions, hunting for a chink in his armor. But Daniel's steadfast faith and integrity left them empty-handed. His only 'crime' was his unwavering devotion to his God, a crime for which they cast him into a den of lions.

But God, ever watchful of His faithful servant, ensured that no harm would befall Daniel. He turned the lion's den into a fortress of safety, making a spectacle of His divine protection and reinforcing the truth that loyalty to God's principles, even in the face of life-threatening danger, never goes unrewarded.

Embracing Humility Amidst Triumphs

As the story of Daniel continues to weave itself, a series of trials and triumphs unfolds. At a juncture, the king of Babylon was gripped by a mysterious dream, its cryptic messages gnawing at his peace of mind. He called upon his wise men, yet none could unravel the enigma. The king, ensnared in frustration, even threatened to execute his wise men.

During this brewing storm, Daniel and his companions sought solace and guidance in prayer. Strengthened by godly revelation, Daniel stepped forward to illuminate the king's troubled mind. His humility echoed in his words as he prepared to reveal the dream's interpretation:

> "But as for me, this secret has not been revealed to me because I have more wisdom than anyone living, but for our sakes who make known the interpretation to the king, and that you may know the thoughts of your heart." Daniel 2:30

Daniel attributed the unraveling of the dream not to his intellect but to God's mercy. His humility shone as he acknowledged his role as merely a vessel for divine wisdom.

Nebuchadnezzar, hearing the words of Daniel, was humbled and overwhelmed. He prostrated himself before Daniel, a moment reminiscent of Pharaoh and Joseph in Egypt:

"Then King Nebuchadnezzar fell on his face, prostrate before Daniel, and commanded that they should present an offering and incense to him. The king answered Daniel, and said, 'Truly your God is the God of Gods, the Lord of kings, and a revealer of secrets, since you could reveal this secret.' Then the king promoted Daniel and gave him many great gifts; and he made him ruler over the whole province of Babylon, and chief administrator over all the wise men of Babylon." Daniel 2:46-48

With Daniel's illumination, Nebuchadnezzar's fear dissolved into reverence, his frustration into faith. He showered Daniel with gifts and praise, elevating him to an esteemed position in the kingdom. Yet, Daniel, even amidst such affluence and authority, remained anchored in humility. He didn't let his triumphs cloud his spirit nor became intoxicated by the adulation he received.

Instead, "Daniel sat at the gate of the king" (Daniel 2:49). This simple yet profound phrase reflects a powerful lesson in humility. Despite his elevated status and the extraordinary gifts he received, Daniel did not lose his sense of self. He refrained from indulging in self-glorification or vanity. Instead, Daniel remained humble, grounded, and centered, preserving his integrity despite his newfound wealth and fame.

In a world that often rewards arrogance and pride, Daniel's story resonates with a timeless truth - that true greatness resides in humility. As we succeed, our ego's gravity should never eclipse our humility's brilliance.

The test of humility is challenging, especially in the face of extraordinary achievements and recognition. Yet, like Daniel, we must prepare ourselves for this test, reminding ourselves that true greatness is less about the accolades we amass and more about the character we maintain.

The Twilight of Daniel's Life

In the shimmering twilight of his life, Daniel's legacy reflected the transformative power of a humble heart. He bore the weight of fame, authority, and wealth with remarkable grace, never succumbing to the seductive lure of ego or the intoxicating aura of power. Amid the tumultuous waves of trials and triumphs, Daniel remained anchored to his core principles, his character unfettered by the changing tides of fortune.

Even as accolades and acclaim came his way, he remained steadfast, as if rooted in the hallowed ground of humility. His life was a testament to the resolute power of character, a beacon illuminating the path of righteous living amid the complex intricacies of worldly success.

Ultimately, Daniel's tale was not one of glory or grandeur but of humility and virtue. His life serves as a potent reminder that true greatness is achieved not by standing above others but by walking among them with grace and humility. Daniel had indeed passed the test of humility and character with flying colors.

From his journey, we glean this timeless wisdom: Stay anchored in your values, remain humble in your triumphs, and stand firm in your faith. When life puts us to the test, our humility, faith, and character will ultimately define our legacy.

Like Daniel, let us strive to meet the trials of life with a resolute heart and a humble spirit. For it is in humility that our true character shines brightest, shaping our lives and the world around us.

Thus, we conclude this chapter on a note of introspection, inviting each of us to reflect upon our lives. Are we ready to embrace humility in the face of success? Are we prepared to stand firm in godly values amidst trials and temptations?

In the final analysis, these questions determine our true character, echoing Daniel's enduring legacy. May his story inspire us as we journey onward, seeking to cultivate a character of integrity, humility, and faith.

Chapter 20

Attitudes to Watch

"Out of suffering have emerged the strongest souls; the most massive characters are seared with scars." - Khalil Gibran

Every moment is a testing ground in the grand theater of life. Each action is a challenge to our character's mettle. The landscape of existence presents trials as numerous as the days of our lives, summoning us to meet them with grace and fortitude.

And each time we falter, we must face the echoes of our missteps, stepping again and again onto the familiar ground of our shortcomings.

This chapter is a guidepost for the wary believer, an intimate conversation about the attitudes we must harbor and the elements of character we should be ever watchful for as we navigate the winding path of life's trials.

A scriptural parallel can be drawn from 1 Peter 1:6-7,

"In this you greatly rejoice, though now for a little while, if need be, you have been grieved by various trials, that the genuineness of your faith, being much more precious than gold that perishes, though it is tested by fire, may be found to praise, honor, and glory at the revelation of Jesus Christ."

Like the purest of gold, our faith is refined by the fiery furnace of trials, and the product of this refinement is a character of more excellent value than any earthly treasure.

However, enduring this process requires a conscious awareness of our attitudes - the spiritual lens through which we perceive and interact with the world. Attitude is the rudder that steers the ship of our character through the tempestuous seas of life's trials.

If the rudder is faulty, the ship may veer off course, succumbing to the storm's fury. But with the rudder held steadfast, anchored by the resilient hands of faith, the ship can endure the storm, emerging on the other side with a reinforced hull and a seasoned crew.

As we prepare to delve deeper into this chapter, remember that trials are a process, and failing is not the end but an invitation to learn and grow. Let us begin by exploring the attitudes that could guide us through this process, enabling us to rise above failure, learn from our mistakes, and become the individuals we are destined to be.

Beware of Dishonoring God

The words echoed in Deuteronomy 8:1-2 are not just historical narratives but divine directives. They're a holy beckoning, urging us to live in obedience and faithfulness:

> *"Every commandment which I command you today you must be careful to observe, that you may live and multiply, and go in and possess the land of which the LORD swore to your fathers. ² And you shall remember that the Lord your God led you all the way these forty years in the wilderness, to humble you and test you, to know what was in your heart, whether you would keep His commandments or not. Deuteronomy 8:1-2*

In His infinite wisdom, the Lord led the children of Israel through the austere wilderness for forty long years. This journey, fraught with trials and tribulations, was not punitive; instead, it was a divine chiseling, a spiritual metamorphosis intended to reveal their true heart, to test their unwavering fidelity to His commands.

This ancient saga is strikingly pertinent to our personal life journeys today. As we traverse the varied landscapes of our lives —from the lush valleys of abundance to the barren deserts of lack—God carefully examines the canvas of our hearts. He watches us, especially at those pivotal junctures when our barns are brimming, our hunger sated, our needs met, and our resources seemingly unending.

At these decisive moments, God looks keenly to discern whether we will continue to obey Him and walk the path of humility or succumb to pride and arrogance, viewing others from a pedestal of self-created superiority.

In these seasons of plenty, we often hear triumphant proclamations: "It is by my own sweat and blood that I have made my wealth, and I determine how to spend it."

While echoing a certain human tenacity and ambition, such statements fail to acknowledge God as the ultimate source of prosperity. They reflect an attitude that dishonors our Lord, disregarding His providence and grace in the process of wealth creation.

To stand up to the test of character, we need to cultivate an attitude of humility, acknowledging that every good thing we have is a blessing from above. In this way, we honor God with our prosperity, attributing our successes not just to our efforts but to His empowering grace.

Beware of the Love of Money

True character, they say, is revealed not in times of comfort but in times of challenge. There are few more significant tests of a person's moral fiber than the wielding of wealth, power, and fame.

Only when individuals ascend to prominence, gain access to influence, and accumulate wealth does their authentic selves surface. Like a relentless tide, it's as if the allure of money washes away superficial pretenses, unveiling what lies beneath.

This truth resonates within the wisdom-laden words of the Apostle Paul to Timothy.

> *Now Godliness with contentment is great gain. For we brought nothing into this world, and it is certain we can carry nothing out. And having food and clothing, with these we shall be content. But those who desire to be rich fall into temptation and a snare, and into many foolish and harmful lusts which drown men in destruction and perdition. For the love of money is a root*

of all kinds of evil, for which some have strayed from the faith in their greediness, and pierced themselves through with many sorrows. But you, O man of God, flee these things and pursue righteousness, Godliness, faith, love, patience, gentleness. 1 Timothy 6:6-11.

The Apostle warned of the perils of the love of money, not money itself. He cautioned against pursuing wealth, knowing it could ensnare even the most devout, leading them astray into the quagmire of greed and despair.

When pursuing wealth becomes the driving force of one's life, we find ourselves adrift in dangerous waters. A person obsessed with money becomes a puppet of their possessions, surrendering their agency to the sway of their fortune.

Such an individual is pitiable, for they've succumbed to an illusory power, confusing the tool with the craftsman. The genuinely wealthy understand that money is not an end but a means—a tool for good or ill, depending on the craftsman's hands.

I recall an incident where a young pastor, whom I had introduced to an apostolic friend overseas, succumbed to the intoxicating allure of money. Upon his return from preaching abroad, he presented me with $5,000. Later, I discovered that my apostolic friend had given him $100,000.

The pastor's greed revealed his true character, so I returned his $5,000, canceled his upcoming appointment, and severed our association. His love for money had overpowered his integrity.

It's disheartening that today, our society often values wealth above character, measuring a person's worth by their financial success rather than their moral standing. But it's important to remember the admonition of Jesus in Luke 12:15, *"Take heed and beware of covetousness, for one's life does not consist in the abundance of the things he possesses."*

Events such as the Covid-19 pandemic strained the world's resources and provided a fresh testing ground for character. Those who maintained their integrity during these trying times passed the test, earning not only their self-respect but also the approval of God.

As we navigate the turbulent waters of this era rife with false doctrines and misconceptions about wealth, let us keep our financial integrity intact. We must serve God not for financial abundance but because we love Him because He is our salvation, our very life.

Remember, if you use power and wealth to hurt others, you set yourself up for a fall and curse your lineage. Your descendants may be forgotten in the annals of history and eternity. We should strive to be remembered not for our wealth or power but for our godly character and acts of kindness, for these are the actual markers of a life well-lived.

Beware of Pride

Pride, a towering sin, casts long shadows that consume even the brightest hearts. Its seductive allure promises power and glory, yet desolation is the only destination it leads to. Ezekiel 28:16 - 17 speaks volumes about the dire consequences of pride:

> *"By the abundance of your trading You became filled with violence within, and you sinned; Therefore I cast you as a*

Beyond the Valley

profane thing Out of the mountain of God; And I destroyed you, O covering cherub, From the midst of the fiery stones. Your heart was lifted up because of your beauty; You corrupted your wisdom for the sake of your splendor; I cast you to the ground, I laid you before kings, that they might gaze at you."

This passage vividly depicts Lucifer's fall from grace, a potent reminder that pride is a dangerous seducer. Once a figure of unparalleled beauty and wisdom, Lucifer became consumed with vanity. His heart, intoxicated by his own magnificence, led him to an audacious, unthinkable path—to attempt to usurp God's authority.

The absurdity of such an endeavor is evident, yet pride blinded him to the futility of his ambition. Can the creature ever hope to surpass the Creator? In his folly, Lucifer lost sight that his beauty, wisdom, and splendor were all gifts from God.

History is replete with tales of pride's disastrous consequences. Take, for example, the emperors of Rome, the Hitlers of Germany, and the Pharaohs of Egypt. These figures once commanded power and fame, their names etched indelibly onto the canvas of history. Yet their hubris, disdain for others, and abuse of power led them to ruin. They are no more, and even their descendants have faded into obscurity.

Their fate serves as a cautionary tale—a stark reminder that how we wield power, wealth, and fame is a testament to our character. We must remain humble, aware that these are merely tools God lent us to be used for the betterment of others and the glory of His name. The cycle of history is unforgiving to those who forget this truth, their names lost in the winds of time, their legacies reduced to tales of warning.

Beware of How You Treat People

Money and power, like a mirror, reflect the depths of a person's soul. They illuminate the character tucked away behind a benign smile, bared for all to see. When fortune favors you, and your words carry the weight of a king's decree, that is not the moment to morph into a harbinger of doom, wielding your influence as a weapon to hunt down those who have wronged you. Destruction is not a mantle to proudly wear.

There comes a moment when the trappings of wealth and power crumble, and in that hour of need, the currency of human compassion becomes invaluable. The imprint of your past interactions with people will echo in how they respond to your plight.

The transient wave of popularity might push you to the forefront of societal attention, but the same sea of voices may one day bellow for your downfall. In times of adversity, when your name is mired in scandal, you get a clear view of your relationships. During these trials, the visage of a true friend materializes - the one who stands by you, not for the allure of your wealth but for the bond that ties you together.

How you treated others in your moments of power and prosperity can significantly shape your place in history or even your legacy in eternity. How you honor the bonds of your past and treat the people from your humble beginnings when fortune smiles at you determines the accurate measure of your character.

Consider the journalist who attempted to tarnish my reputation, wielding his pen like a poisoned dagger. I warned him that if he used his position for malevolence, it would inevitably be stripped from him. Time proved this prophecy to be true. Though he sought forgiveness, the consequences of his actions could not be undone.

People crave recognition. Leaders, therefore, must exercise caution and empathy in their dealings with their subordinates. You will find your greatest reward in fostering their growth, sometimes allowing them to outshine you. Consider the story of Elijah and Elisha - Elijah mentored Elisha, yet Elisha performed greater miracles than he did.

Our successors stand on our shoulders; their vision extends beyond ours. Never let your ego stand in the way of their ascent.

Beware of the temptation that power brings. It can fill one with the desire for petty revenge, to settle scores from bygone days. To act on such impulses is to let power and money blind you and to lose sight of your humanity.

Upon his release from prison, Nelson Mandela did not seek vengeance against those who mistreated him. He understood the power of forgiveness. His words are an invaluable lesson for us all:

"As I stand before the door to my freedom, I realize that if I don't leave behind me my bitterness, and my unforgiveness, I will walk through these doors to freedom and still be in prison."

Such are the ways of wisdom, ever cautioning us against the intoxicating pull of power and money, reminding us of the value of humility, compassion, and love for our fellow beings.

Chapter 21

Modeling Christian Character

"Our character is what we do when we think no one is looking." - H. Jackson Brown Jr.

Christian character is not an outward adornment to be admired in passing. It is not a flashy car, a designer suit, or an exquisitely crafted piece of jewelry. Instead, it is an inner fortress, a living testament of the indwelling Spirit of Christ.

In a world fascinated by surfaces, the Apostle Paul provides a poignant counterpoint in his first epistle to Timothy. "Let no one despise your youth," he says, "but be an example to the believers in word, in conduct, in love, in spirit, in faith, in purity." (1 Timothy 4:12)

Being an example to the believers is no small task. Shining a light into the darkness is easier than illuminating the day. To model Christian character among fellow believers, one must rise above the ordinary; one must radiate the extraordinary.

And the instruction of Jesus rings true: "Let your light so shine before men," not through ostentatious prayers or loud proclamations of faith, but through the quiet yet powerful display of character.

In its impetuosity, youth tend to gravitate towards the first half of the apostle's message, shirking any notion of inferiority due to age. Yet, in their eagerness to establish their standing, they overlook the deeper, more profound aspect of Paul's advice - the charge to reflect Christ-like character. The standard set forth is indeed lofty, for it is Jesus, Himself.

Asserting one's place is about something other than being the loudest, the most tech-savvy, or the most adept at social media. It lies instead in demonstrating Christ's character.

In his letter to the Philippians, Paul invites them to follow his example, cautioning them to be wary of those who live contrary to the teachings of Christ. He condemns those who exalt earthly desires, living as if their stomach was their god, and finding pride in their shameful actions.

> *Brethren, join in following my example, and note those who so walk, as you have us for a pattern For many walk, of whom I have told you often, and now tell you even weeping, that they are the enemies of the cross of Christ: whose end is destruction, whose God is their belly, and whose glory is in their shame—who set their mind on earthly things. Philippians 3:17-19*

His heartfelt prayer is that those who follow his lead will not be led astray. As echoed in his epistle to Titus, the Apostle extends this charge of modeling Christian character to women of all ages within the church.

But as for you, speak the things which are proper for sound doctrine: that the older men be sober, reverent, temperate, sound in faith, in love, in patience; the older women likewise, that they be reverent in behavior, not slanderers, not given to much wine, teachers of good things— that they admonish the young women to love their husbands, to love their children, to be discreet, chaste, homemakers, good, obedient to their own husbands, that the word of God may not be blasphemed. Likewise, exhort the young men to be sober-minded, in all things showing yourself to be a pattern of good works; in doctrine showing integrity, reverence, incorruptibility, sound speech that cannot be condemned, that one who is an opponent may be ashamed, having nothing evil to say of you. Titus 2:1-8

In this exhortation, we understand that God expects us not to showcase vanity, pride, or malice but to become a living blueprint of good works. In this imitation of Christ's character, we fulfill our role as His disciples and truly reflect His light into the world.

Path to Modeling Christian Character

The path to modeling Christian character is not strewn with flowers but instead lined with thorns, and it takes a commitment that reaches the depths of our being. How, then, do we embark on this journey?

We Need More of Jesus.

In the Apostle Paul's letter to the Philippians, he speaks a profound truth: "I can do all things through Christ who strengthens me." (Philippians 4:13)

In this simple yet profound declaration, he lays bare the very heart of Christian character - an unwavering reliance on Jesus Christ. The power to display the virtues of Christian character does not come from within us; instead, it is a divine outpouring from Christ Himself.

The more we imbibe the nature of Jesus, the more His radiance shines through us. He is the wellspring of all virtues, the reservoir of all goodness. His divine nature fills the Godhead to overflow. It is in Him and through Him that we can attain completeness.

Echoing this truth, the writer of the book of Hebrews urges us to continually fix our eyes on Jesus, the author, and perfecter of our faith.

> "Therefore, we also, since we are surrounded by so great a cloud of witnesses, let us lay aside every weight, and the sin which so easily ensnares us, and let us run with endurance the race that is set before us, looking unto Jesus, the author and finisher of our faith, who for the joy that was set before Him endured the cross, despising the shame, and has sat down at the right hand of the throne of God." Hebrews 12:1-2

The apostle's message here is twofold. Firstly, we are encouraged to shed all the weights and sins that hold us back, anything that entangles us and hinders our progress.

Secondly, we are urged to steadfastly gaze upon Jesus, to set our eyes on Him who bore the cross for our sakes. His example is the shining beacon guiding us on our journey.

Indeed, the key to modeling Christian character is not found in an outward display of piety or a mechanical following of religious rules. It is about an inward transformation, a heart that yearns for more of Jesus. And as we yearn for and seek Him, His divine strength empowers us, His love molds us, and His grace enables us to reflect His character to the world.

We Need Greater Faith.

In the letter to the Hebrews, the author lays out a profound truth:

"But without faith it is impossible to please Him, for he who comes to God must believe that He is, and that He is a rewarder of those who diligently seek Him." Hebrews 11:6

The believer's journey commences with faith in Jesus Christ and continues with faith in the Godhead – Father, Son, and Holy Spirit. God delights in our faith and rewards it, as demonstrated in the lives of Joseph, David, Esther, Daniel, and all the other faithful chronicled in Hebrews Chapter 11.

The faith we invest in God's character guides our decisions. In the face of insult, we maintain our silence, knowing that vengeance is God's province. This is faith in action, confidence in God's power to defend us, open new doors, and aid us in making the right choices.

We Need More of the Word of God.

Paul wrote to Timothy,

"All Scripture is given by inspiration of God, and is profitable for doctrine, for reproof, for correction, for instruction in righteousness, that the man of God may be complete, thoroughly equipped for every good work." 2 Timothy 3:16-17

No sphere of life is left untouched by the Bible. It provides instruction for every situation and every role - whether for married couples, parents, craftsmen, doctors, engineers, teachers, or entrepreneurs. It offers guidance for all of life's endeavors.

Through the Word of God, we are transformed into the likeness of Jesus Christ, our Lord. As Paul entreats in Romans 12:1-2,

> "I beseech you therefore, brethren, by the mercies of God, that you present your bodies a living sacrifice, holy, acceptable to God, which is your reasonable service. And do not be conformed to this world, but be transformed by the renewing of your mind, that you may prove what is that good and acceptable and perfect will of God."

Allow the Word to transform you. You cannot remain in Christ and still harbor a carnal mindset. Change the way you think, discard the worldly mentality, and live like King David, who said, *"Thy word have I hid in my heart that I might not sin against You."* (Psalm 119:11) The Word of God is the compass that keeps us on the straight path, even in the face of temptation.

We Need a Daily Practice of Prayer

In his letter to the Thessalonians, Paul admonishes, "Pray without ceasing." (1 Thessalonians 5:17)

We should add fasting to our prayers, as it injects spiritual power into our supplications and helps us overcome temptations.

Consider the exchange Jesus had with His disciples in Matthew 17:17-21:

> *Then Jesus answered and said, "O faithless and perverse generation, how long shall I be with you? How long shall I bear with you? Bring him here to Me." And Jesus rebuked the demon, and it came out of him; and the child was cured from that very hour. Then the disciples came to Jesus privately and said, "Why could we not cast it out?" So Jesus said to them, "Because of your unbelief; for assuredly, I say to you, if you have faith as a mustard seed, you will say to this mountain, 'Move from here to there,' and it will move; and nothing will be impossible for you. However, this kind does not go out except by prayer and fasting."*

After the transfiguration, Jesus used a moment of failure on the part of His disciples to teach about the importance of prayer and fasting in overcoming spiritual hurdles. Jesus underscores the fact that there are spiritual battles that can only be won through a combination of prayer and fasting.

Fasting is more than an emergency measure taken in the hour of need. Instead, it should be a lifestyle, a regular practice that sharpens our spiritual sensitivity and empowers us to conquer challenges. It is a warfare strategy against every evil habit that seeks to enslave us. The struggle experienced during fasting should remind us of the spiritual battle at hand. When fasting becomes a lifestyle, it unlocks spiritual power beyond our comprehension.

The Demand for Personal Decisiveness

In the book of Daniel, we find a testament of conviction,

> "But Daniel purposed in his heart that he would not defile himself with the portion of the king's delicacies, nor with the wine which he drank; therefore, he requested of the chief of the eunuchs that he might not defile himself." (Daniel 1:8)

Knowledge alone doesn't bring change. It is the decision to act, to choose the right path, that brings about transformation. This decision is an exercise of your will, steered by the Holy Spirit.

Daniel didn't wait for the day of temptation to make his decision. He chose ahead of time, as did Joseph when he decided not to sin against God. David decided not to harm God's anointed. These were personal decisions made in anticipation of future temptations.

In the wisdom-filled book of Proverbs, we read, *"He who walks with wise men will be wise, but the companion of fools will be destroyed."* (Proverbs 13:20)

Choose to journey with the wise, not the foolish. Evil communication corrupts good manners. As iron sharpens iron, align yourself with those who refine your character. Do not align with those who pull you into sin, but with those who urge you towards righteousness.

The Call to Personal Action

Deciding without acting is as ineffective as not deciding at all. Words without action are but hollow sounds echoing into the void. Ephesians 4:20-24 tells us,

> "But you have not so learned Christ, if indeed you have heard Him and have been taught by Him, as the truth is in Jesus: that you put off, concerning your former conduct, the old man which grows corrupt according to the deceitful lusts, and be renewed in the spirit of your mind, and that you put on the new man which was created according to God, in true righteousness and holiness."

This scripture urges us towards an intentional act of transformation, a 'putting off' and a 'putting on.' Cast off your former self, your old habits of anger, vengeance, and immorality. Don't defend wrongdoing in your life, attributing it to familial tendencies or inherited character.

If something is contrary to God's word, we must oppose it. In place of the old, clothe yourself in the new nature, the new image given by Christ. Live not in past mistakes but in God's present righteousness and holiness. This is a deliberate action, an active step towards embodying the Christian character.

The Call for Unwavering Determination

The Apostle Paul shares a powerful metaphor in his first letter to the Corinthians, offering both instruction and encouragement:

> "Do you not know that those who run in a race all run, but one receives the prize? Run in such a way that you may obtain it. And everyone who competes for the prize is temperate in all things. Now they do it to obtain a perishable crown, but we for an imperishable crown. Therefore I run thus: not with uncertainty. Thus I fight: not as one who beats the air. But I discipline my body and bring it into subjection, lest, when I have preached to others, I myself should become disqualified." 1 Corinthians 9:24-27

This verse calls us to personal discipline and an unyielding determination. It compels us to rein in our baser instincts, to refuse to let our fleshly desires command our actions. Instead, we are to deny these ephemeral cravings and cultivate the spirit's yearnings under the Holy Spirit's transformative influence.

The Pursuit of Perfection

In light of our human fragility, Jesus's command might appear daunting:

> You have heard that it was said, 'You shall love your neighbor and hate your enemy.' But I say to you, love your enemies, bless those who curse you, do good to those who hate you, and pray for those who spitefully use you and persecute you, that you may be sons of your Father in heaven; for He makes His sun rise on the evil and on the good, and sends rain on the just and on the unjust. For if you love those who love you, what reward have you? Do not even the tax collectors do the same? And if you greet your brethren only, what do you do more than others? Do

not even the tax collectors do so? ***Therefore you shall be perfect, just as your Father in heaven is perfect.*** Matthew 5:43 - 48

After an exhortation to love our enemies and pray for those who persecute us, this verse invites us to an all-encompassing love and impartial kindness that mirrors God's generosity.

Jesus would not have asked this of us if it were beyond our reach.

Thus, let us not place limits on the extent to which we can embody Christian character. God demonstrated His perfection in Jesus without reservation. And if God were to find someone on earth who mirrors Jesus, imagine the joy and delight it would bring Him! So, let us strive towards this lofty goal of perfection, modeling our character after our Lord Jesus Christ.

The Reward of Character

In the grand tapestry of life, character shines through as the golden thread, defining and distinguishing us. Character is rewarded by God, who steadfastly delivers the righteous in times of calamity—even when the very calamity emanates from Him due to a nation's transgressions.

In His messages to the prophet Ezekiel, God's profound regard for character is explicit:

"The word of the LORD came again to me, saying: 'Son of man, when a land sins against Me by persistent unfaithfulness, I will stretch out My hand against it; I will cut off its supply of bread, send famine on it, and cut off man and beast from it. Even if

these three men, Noah, Daniel, and Job, were in it, they would deliver only themselves by their righteousness... If I cause wild beasts to pass through the land, and they empty it, and make it so desolate that no man may pass through because of the beasts, even though these three men were in it... they would deliver neither sons nor daughters; only they would be delivered, and the land would be desolate.'" Ezekiel 14:12-16

Here, God affirms His deep respect for three virtuous men —Noah, Daniel, and Job—promising them deliverance during times of crisis. Their righteousness, their virtuous character, is their shield. As the Noahs, Daniels, and Davids of our times, it is incumbent upon us to plead with the Lord to preserve us and our lands. We are privileged to emulate these stalwart men of faith.

The Apostle Paul, writing to the church in Rome, calls us to walk in the character of Christ, to embody His virtues:

"Let us walk honestly, as in the day; not in rioting and drunkenness, not in chambering and wantonness, not in strife and envying. But put ye on the Lord Jesus Christ, and make not provision for the flesh, to fulfill the lusts thereof." Romans 13:13-14

In another scripture, we are exhorted to don the attributes of Christ like a garment:

"Therefore, as the elect of God, holy and beloved, put on tender mercies, kindness, humility, meekness, longsuffering... But above all these things put on love, which is the bond of perfection..." Colossians 3:12-17

Our character matters. Our standing with God matters. The Lord not only recognizes our character, but He also safeguards it. Amid God's judgment, the upright find refuge in Him.

Character seems to epitomize a life of faith, a life of obedience to God's word, and a life devoted to God. The saints we've studied in previous parts of this book —including The Test of Faith and The Test of Love—display remarkable character, as do the obedient souls in a hypothetical Test of Obedience. These attributes—faith, love, obedience—intersect and mirror each other, culminating in the character one manifests in life.

May we all have the privilege of God Himself validating our character, and may we strive each day to emulate the very nature of Christ in our thoughts, words, and deeds.

Prayer

Heavenly Father,

Let your Spirit move with grace and power in the quiet spaces between these words and our hearts. We thank you for the lessons we have learned, the wisdom we have gleaned, and the growth we have experienced. We thank you for your unwavering faithfulness, infinite love, and the godly image of character you have set before us.

Lord, we ask that you fortify our faith so that we may stand firm even amidst the strongest tempests. Deepen our love so that it might mirror your own boundless love, reaching out to touch and transform the lives around us. And mold our character, Lord, to reflect your goodness and righteousness in all we do.

As we continue our journey, let us remember the truths we have discovered, the strengths we have recognized, and the weaknesses we have confronted. Help us to apply these truths in our daily lives, strengthening our resolve to walk in faith, live in love, and act with unwavering character.

May our lives be a living testimony to Your grace, a beacon of Your love, and a reflection of Your character. And when we are tested, as we surely will be, grant us the strength to endure, the courage to persevere, and the wisdom to understand that we are drawn closer to You in these moments of testing.

In Jesus' name, we pray.

Amen.

Epilogue

As we draw the curtains on this spiritual exploration, I hope your heart has been touched, your spirit enriched, and your understanding deepened. We embarked on a journey together, traversing the terrain of faith, love, and character. When tested, we have seen how these elements can refine us, transforming our lives into a living testimony of God's grace and power.

In each chapter, we've seen reflections of our own journeys, recognizing ourselves in the stories of Daniel's resolve, Paul's determination, and Christ's perfect love. Their lives, interwoven with scripture, have imparted valuable lessons, reminding us that our faith, love, and character are not just personal traits but gifts by the Holy Spirit designed to draw us closer to God and become a reflection of Jesus in this world.

As Jesus said in Matthew 5:14: *"You are the light of the world. A city that is set on a hill cannot be hidden."*

We've grappled with tests, trials, and tribulations, only to find that they are not meant to break us but to make us — to mold us into the individuals God destined us to be. Although often uncomfortable, the pressure and heat of life's furnace are essential processes in shaping us, akin to the transformation of rough carbon into a sparkling diamond.

May the wisdom and insights shared in these pages not be merely read but absorbed and lived out in your everyday life. I pray that as you close this book, you do not close your heart to the truths contained within but continue to reflect, grow, and bear the fruit of righteousness. May your faith, love, and character continue to be tested, and through each test, may they be strengthened.

About the Author

With over four decades of Ministry behind him, Archbishop Nicholas Duncan-Williams is the Presiding Archbishop and General Overseer of Action Chapel International (ACI), headquartered in Accra, Ghana, and United Denominations of Action Chapel International, which has over 150 affiliates and branch churches located in North America, Europe, Asia, and Africa.

Archbishop Duncan-Williams is also the Founder and Chairman of Nicholas Duncan-Williams Ministries (formerly Prayer Summit International), which hosts prayer summits around the globe, bringing revival to international cities through corporate and intercessory prayer and training.

With a unique anointing in prayer and intercession, Archbishop is recognized by many leaders in the body of Christ as the "Apostle of Strategic Prayer."

Having gained accreditation and respect from recognized church leaders, God has used him to counsel and speak into the lives of world leaders while still maintaining his touch with the everyday person. As a result, he is affectionately called "Papa" by many.

1 million strong

Global Prayer Community
Join today at http://ndwministries.org/1-million-strong/

Archbishop N. Duncan-Williams

Free Instant Access to:

- Financial Freedom Prayer Declaration
- Discover The Secrets to Effective Prayer (course)
- Breakthrough in the Spiritual Realm (audio)

Made in the USA
Middletown, DE
08 July 2024